YORK FILM NOTES

Lawrence of Arabia

Director
David Lean

Note by Martin Stollery

Longman   York Press

York Press
322 Old Brompton Road, London SW5 9JH

Pearson Education Limited
Edinburgh Gate, Harlow, Essex CM20 2JE, United Kingdom
Associated companies, branches and representatives throughout
the world

All stills and screenplay extracts are reproduced by courtesy of
Columbia Tristar International and are © Columbia Tristar International

First published 2000

ISBN 0-582-43192-1

Designed by Vicki Pacey
Phototypeset by Gem Graphics, Trenance, Mawgan Porth, Cornwall
Colour reproduction and film output by Spectrum Colour
Printed in Great Britain by Henry Ling Limited, Dorchester, Dorset

contents

author of this note Martin Stollery is Senior Lecturer
in Film Studies at Southampton Institute, specialising in British cinema,
Middle Eastern cinemas, and cinematic representations of the Middle
East. His PhD is from the University of Warwick. Publications include
*Alternative Empires: European Modernist Cinemas and Cultures of
Imperialism* (Exeter University Press) and *Youssef Chahine's L'Émigré*
(Flicks Books).

NOTE: There are slight discrepancies between the dialogue in the
film script and the lines delivered by the actors in the film. Also the
spelling of names may vary between the script and this Note.

background

trailer

Romantic landscapes, august landscapes – one has seen these often enough on the screen. This is something else. The sun rising on the rim of blood-orange sand; dust storms like the smoke-trails of a djinn; the shapes of infinity, the colours of heat – I think it is the first time for the cinema to communicate ecstasy.

Dilys Powell, The Sunday Times, 16 December 1962

Here is an epic with intellect behind it ... Who on earth has wrought this miracle? The makers. Producer Sam Spiegel is a man of culture as well as finance. David Lean is a director who goes out to the wild place to meditate on his films, much as prophets used to contemplate unworldly things. Scriptwriter Robert Bolt is our subtlest playwright of men's emotions. And I think that Allah, in the shape of F.A. Young's Technicolor camerawork, poured down his blessing for the two years of filming. An unbeatable team!

Alexander Walker, Evening Standard, 13 December 1962

[D]ull, overlong and coldly impersonal ...

Andrew Sarris, The Village Voice, 20 December 1962

The sheer logistics of *Lawrence* ... cannot support the luxury of a directorial point of view ... whatever artistic sensibility [director David Lean] once possessed is safely embalmed in the tomb of the impersonal cinema.

Andrew Sarris, The American Cinema, 1968

[O]ne of the film's faults is that cinemagoers who don't know about the Lawrence legend may be confused. The pic starts, for instance, with his fatal motorcycle crash in England. This could seem a puzzling, irrelevant scene for those who do not know how this strange soldier met his end.

Variety, 19 December 1962

In the performance Peter O'Toole gives, there seem to be at least ten incompatible men living under the same skin, and two or three women as well ... When he puts on a sherif's robes for the first time and does an entranced ballet with himself in the desert, it made me think more than ever that one of the reasons for Lawrence's passion for Arab life might well have been that it allowed him to wear a skirt.

Penelope Gilliat, The Observer, 16 December 1962

[After the London première] Noël Coward said that had Peter O'Toole been any prettier, the film would have to have been called 'Florence of Arabia'.

Kevin Brownlow, David Lean, 1997

If one measure of a film's greatness is its power to affect the lives of those who see it, then *Lawrence of Arabia* must be the best film I know.

Janet Maslin, New York Times, 29 January 1989

reading lawrence

In 1999 the BFI (British Film Institute) compiled a list of the hundred best British films. *Lawrence of Arabia* came third. *Lawrence* is now an established classic, part of the history of both British and Hollywood cinema. It can be seen as a British film insofar as a significant proportion of the film's cast and crew were British. They brought with them skills and attitudes arising from their previous experience within the British film industry. Yet from another perspective *Lawrence* is a Hollywood film. It is an outstanding example of the cycle of Hollywood film epics produced between the late 1950s and early 1960s (see Filmography). It was partly financed and distributed by Columbia, a major Hollywood studio (see Industrial).

Lawrence contains some unforgettable moments which have permanently lodged themselves in the memories of many people who have seen the film. These include sequences such as the arrival through a mirage of Sherif Ali, played by Omar Sharif, for his first encounter with Lawrence (see Realism, exoticism, and subjectivity). However, the historical events referred to in *Lawrence* may now seem quite distant from us. When *Lawrence* was first released in 1962, the following title card was designed to precede the film when shown in the Far East and Latin America. It outlines the film's historical context, which today's audiences might not be familiar with:

> In 1916, Britain and France were allied against the Germans in a struggle which is known as World War One. Turkey, which for centuries dominated the Middle East, aligned itself on the side of Germany. It became vital to the British strategy that the Arab tribes, living under Turkish rule, be united. An obscure Lieutenant with the British forces in Egypt was destined to become the spark that kindled the Arab Revolt in the desert. His name was T.E. Lawrence

T.E. Lawrence's exploits as a leader of the Arab revolt were widely publicised in Britain and America immediately after the First World War (see Production history: Script). Romanticised descriptions of Lawrence's heroic adventures in the Arabian desert provided a colourful, exotic alternative to bleak accounts of trench warfare in Europe. Lawrence's memoir of his time in the desert, *The Seven Pillars of Wisdom* (1935), was widely read. It helped to sustain his legend whilst also representing him as a complex, enigmatic character. Beginning with Alexander Korda in the 1930s, several producers attempted to set up film projects about Lawrence. Until Sam Spiegel did so, none were successful in carrying these through to completion.

Lawrence premièred towards the end of 1962. In 1963 it was rewarded with seven Oscars. Producer Sam Spiegel collected the award for best picture, David Lean for best director, Freddie Young for cinematography, and Anne Coates for editing. Art and set decoration, sound and music were also awarded Oscars. *Lawrence* was an imaginative, inventive, technically sophisticated production which effectively coordinated the skills of a range of top film making talents (see Industrial). Over the years different audiences have enjoyed *Lawrence* for a variety of different reasons (see Audience). In 1989, after several years' work, a restored version of *Lawrence* was rereleased in cinemas and subsequently issued on video (see Production history: Reediting and restoration).

With the publication in 1999 of Steven Caton's book on the film, *Lawrence* joined that very small group of films which have had full length academic studies devoted to them. This is further evidence of *Lawrence*'s firmly established classic status. Not all film critics and theorists praise the film, however. Some, like Andrew Sarris, find *Lawrence* 'overlong' and 'coldly impersonal'. Despite granting permission for the filming of *Lawrence* to take place in Jordan, the Jordanian government banned the film. Many other Arab governments followed suit. In *Unthinking Eurocentrism* (1994), their standard text on cinematic representations of the non-Western world, Ella Shohat and Robert Stam criticise *Lawrence* for its 'orientalism' (see Ideology: Orientalism). Steven Caton's book disagrees with some of the points made by Shohat and Stam. *Lawrence* continues to raise many issues worth analysing and debating.

key players' biographies

Many highly skilled actors and production staff were involved in the lengthy, demanding process of making *Lawrence of Arabia*. Adrian Turner's book on the making of the film contains the most extensive credits list currently available. Many different people made diverse contributions to the making of the film. To take one example, former British Foreign Office minister Anthony Nutting, credited as director of public relations, was a respected figure within Middle Eastern diplomatic circles. He was essential to negotiations with the Jordanian government which led to permission being granted to film in or near the actual locations Lawrence had travelled across and fought in. Many other people made important contributions to *Lawrence*. The brief biographies which follow profile only a small number of them. The production workers selected here are those who worked on aspects of the film discussed in more detail later in this Note.

biographies

PRODUCER

By the time he came to produce *Lawrence of Arabia* Sam Spiegel was widely travelled, spoke many languages, and had an extensive network of film industry contacts. Before establishing himself as one of Hollywood's leading independent producers, he worked in various capacities for major studios like MGM (Metro-Goldwyn-Mayer) and Universal. On the production side he gained experience as a script advisor, searching out plays which could be adapted into film scripts. On the distribution side he helped to supervise the cutting and dubbing of Hollywood films to make them suitable for European audiences. Spiegel was also an impressive deal maker and negotiator, and these skills were essential for obtaining permission to film *Lawrence* in Jordan.

Spiegel's deal making skills and his experience of various aspects of the Hollywood film industry equipped him well for the shift towards independent production which occurred after the end of the Second World War (see Industrial). He formed an independent production company, Horizon Pictures, with director John Huston. Horizon's successful productions included *The African Queen* (John Huston, 1951) and *On the Waterfront* (Elia Kazan, 1954). David Lean's first film with Horizon was *The Bridge on the River Kwai* (1957). He had not been Spiegel's first choice, and was offered the film because other directors Spiegel considered more suitable were not available.

After *Kwai*'s tremendous success, Spiegel was keen to work with Lean again. They eventually settled on *Lawrence* as their next project. *Kwai*'s success considerably boosted Spiegel's and Lean's reputations. This enabled Spiegel to attract significant financial backing for *Lawrence*, and to bring together some of the top professionals within the industry to work on the project (see Industrial). Spiegel went on to produce other significant films in the 1960s, for example *The Chase* (Arthur Penn, 1966), but *Lawrence* was the high point of his career.

DIRECTOR

David Lean was a highly regarded film editor before he became a director. He edited a number of significant British films during the 1930s and early

biographies

1940s. These included *As You Like It* (Paul Czinner, 1937), *Pygmalion* (Anthony Asquith, 1938), and *49th Parallel* (Michael Powell, 1941). Lean's first film as director was *In Which We Serve* (co-director Noël Coward, 1942). His three subsequent films were adaptations of Coward's plays. The one remembered with most affection today is *Brief Encounter* (1945). With *Great Expectations* (1946) and *Oliver Twist* (1948) Lean turned to Charles Dickens adaptations. He continued to direct successful films throughout the 1950s.

Lean's career took a new turn when he joined forces with independent Hollywood producer Sam Spiegel to make the Second World War epic *The Bridge on the River Kwai* (1957). *Lawrence of Arabia*, his next film, was followed by *Doctor Zhivago* (1965), *Ryan's Daughter* (1970) and finally, after a long break from feature film making, *A Passage to India* (1984). *Doctor Zhivago* and *Ryan's Daughter* were, like *Lawrence*, scripted by Robert Bolt and shot by Freddie Young.

Doctor Zhivago was an adaptation of the famous novel of the same name by Boris Pasternak. Similarly, *A Passage to India* was based on a novel by E.M. Forster. All of Lean's later epic films were set in exotic locations such as Burma, the Middle East, and India. Within certain limits, they feature complex representations of non-Western characters. These include Sherif Ali in *Lawrence* and Colonel Saito in *Kwai*. Lean was insistent that the similarities as well as the differences between Saito and his British antagonist Colonel Nicholson should be highlighted in *Kwai*. *Lawrence* represents the similarities and differences between Sherif Ali and Lawrence in a similar fashion (see Character transformations).

STARS

Peter O'Toole trained as an actor at RADA (the Royal Academy of Dramatic Arts). He was a rising young star of British theatre when cast in the lead role of *Lawrence of Arabia*. O'Toole appeared in a few films prior to *Lawrence*, but this was by far his most important role. Lean spotted him in *The Day they Robbed the Bank of England* (John Guillermin, 1960). In his book on *Lawrence* Steven Caton argues that O'Toole's theatrical training is evident in his performance in the film. Caton suggests that this enhances the idea within the film's narrative that Lawrence is a performer, an

Peter O'Toole as
Lawrence

'Florence of Arabia'

exhibitionist, who delights in playing a role for the media and for various audiences (see Performance and dialogue).

O'Toole has unusual physical characteristics for a male epic film hero. He is tall, thin, slightly built, has delicate features and sensitive eyes. His body and overall demeanour are quite different from the muscular frames and rugged faces of more conventional male epic stars like Charlton Heston and Kirk Douglas (see Production history: Casting, and Cultural contexts: Audience). Lean saw sexual ambiguity as a central element within O'Toole's star image, and said that he purposefully tried to capitalise on this in *Lawrence*. At the film's London première Noël Coward immediately picked up on this with his quip about 'Florence of Arabia'. O'Toole in the role of Lawrence is a star well suited to *Lawrence*'s exploration of what men should be and do, how they should relate to each other, and how they should be looked at (see Genre: The male epic).

After *Lawrence* O'Toole played a number of roles which similarly placed him as a Westerner in an exotic non-Western context. *Lord Jim* (Richard Brooks, 1964), set in the Far East and based upon a novel by Joseph Conrad was, like *Lawrence*, photographed by Freddie Young. In *The Last Emperor* (Bernardo Bertolucci, 1987) O'Toole was cast as the tutor of the last Chinese emperor. Both films draw upon the association between O'Toole, exotic locations and imperial themes established by *Lawrence*. O'Toole has appeared in numerous other films since *Lawrence*. He was cast with Omar Sharif again in *The Night of the Generals* (Anatole Litvak, 1967) in an attempt to recapture the special chemistry between the two *Lawrence* stars. O'Toole has also continued to work in the theatre.

Omar Sharif was in his early twenties when he made his debut in the Egyptian film *The Blazing Sun* (Youssef Chahine, 1954). He went on to star in a number of Egyptian as well as French films of the 1950s and 1960s. *Lawrence of Arabia* was his first Hollywood role and the film which brought him international attention. Sharif comes from the sophisticated, cosmopolitan city of Alexandria in Egypt, quite unlike the Bedouin character Sherif Ali he plays in *Lawrence*. Nevertheless casting Sharif, an Arab actor, to play a serious Arab character in a major Hollywood production was a significant development in the early 1960s. The usual practice was for Arab roles to be played by white American or European actors (see Production history: Casting). Examples from late 1950s and 1960s epics include Hugh Griffith playing Arab roles in *Ben-Hur* (William Wyler, 1959) and *Exodus* (Otto Preminger, 1960), and Laurence Olivier as the Sudanese Mahdi in *Khartoum* (Basil Dearden, 1966).

After *Lawrence* Sharif was cast in a variety of non-white 'ethnic' roles. He played an Armenian in *The Fall of the Roman Empire* (Anthony Mann, 1964), and a Mongol in *Genghis Khan* (Henry Levin, 1964). However, Sharif was interestingly cast as the Russian hero of *Doctor Zhivago*, the film Lean directed after *Lawrence*. Numerous other roles in Hollywood, European and Egyptian films followed. During the late 1980s and 1990s Sharif starred primarily in Egyptian films, such as *The Puppet Player* (Hani Lachine, 1989) and *War on the Land of Egypt* (Salah Abou Seif, 1991). At the same time he also continued to act in Hollywood films, for example *The Thirteenth Warrior* (John McTiernan, 1999). Sharif's career is significant for the extent to which he has worked successfully across several different national contexts.

SCRIPTWRITERS

The British dramatist Robert Bolt received screen credit for *Lawrence of Arabia*'s script. Initially a school teacher, he gradually branched out into writing radio and stage plays. *Flowering Cherry* was staged in London in 1958 and ran successfully for over a year. It was followed by another big hit, *A Man for All Seasons*, a historical drama about the political and ethical conflict between Sir Thomas More and King Henry VIII. This play was later made into a film directed by Fred Zinnemann in 1966.

Bolt was new to scriptwriting when Sam Spiegel recruited him to work on *Lawrence*. Bolt's collaboration with Lean proved so fruitful that they worked on two more films together, *Doctor Zhivago* and *Ryan's Daughter*. After this Bolt continued to write for theatre and television as well as scripting films. Some of these, such as *The Bounty* (Roger Donaldson, 1984) and *The Mission* (Roland Joffé, 1986), explore the issue of encounters between Western and non-Western cultures which is central to *Lawrence*.

The American scriptwriter Michael Wilson produced the first version of the *Lawrence of Arabia* script for Lean and Spiegel. Wilson had collaborated with this producer-director team before, making a substantial contribution to the script for *The Bridge on the River Kwai*. In the 1940s and 1950s Wilson had established himself as a leading Hollywood scriptwriter. His credits included *It's a Wonderful Life* (Frank Capra, 1946) and *A Place in the Sun* (George Stevens, 1951).

The anti-Communist witch hunt in 1950s Hollywood disrupted Wilson's career, and resulted in his being 'blacklisted'. He was denied employment or screen credit for films he did work on. Wilson moved into independent production (see Industrial). He wrote the script for the left-wing film *Salt of the Earth* (Paul Jerrico, 1953). This was blocked from distribution in America. Because of the blacklist, Wilson did not receive screen credit for his work on *Friendly Persuasion* (William Wyler, 1956). Some film historians have argued that this was also a reason why he did not receive any screen credit for *Kwai* or *Lawrence* (see Production history: Script).

CINEMATOGRAPHER

The beginning of Freddie Young's career as a cinematographer dates back to the 1920s. He worked on many distinguished British films during the 1930s and 1940s, including *Victoria the Great* (Herbert Wilcox, 1937) and *49th Parallel* (Michael Powell, 1941). Young was one of the first cinematographers to become expert in and to experiment with the use of Technicolor. Prior to *Lawrence of Arabia* he worked on many Hollywood productions, establishing a reputation as one of the world's best cinematographers. Young's credits during the 1950s include the biblical epic *Solomon and Sheba* (King Vidor, 1959) and the acclaimed *Lust for Life* (Vincente Minnelli, 1956). He was at the top of his profession when he worked on *Lawrence*. Young collaborated with Lean again on *Doctor Zhivago* and *Ryan's Daughter*.

Lust for Life was a biopic starring Kirk Douglas as the famous Dutch artist Vincent Van Gogh. Young's Technicolor cinematography for this film stretched the boundaries of the use of colour in Hollywood cinema. Rather than adhering to strictly realistic norms, the representation of Van Gogh's environment in *Lust for Life* is modelled on the artist's vivid, colourful paintings. Young's cinematography expresses Van Gogh's subjectivity. The painter's feelings and emotions are reflected in the world around him. *Lawrence* called for similar experimentation with cinematic technique. As in *Lust for Life*, Young's cinematography in *Lawrence* represents both a realistic, objective world and aspects of the protagonist's inner world (see Cinematography and mise-en-scène, and Realism, exoticism, and subjectivity).

EDITOR

Before working on *Lawrence* Anne Coates's editing experience was mainly with British rather than international films (see Production history). Her credits prior to *Lawrence* include the British films *The Horse's Mouth* (Ronald Neame, 1958) and *Tunes of Glory* (Ronald Neame, 1960). Coates has discussed her work on *Lawrence* in several interviews, and has talked about the importance of the editing for pacing this lengthy film. Decisions such as how exactly to time the famous cut between Lawrence blowing out a match in Cairo and the sun slowly rising over a desert horizon were crucial to making these editing effects work (see Editing).

Coates has revealed that some of the more unconventional editing in *Lawrence* was influenced by the French New Wave films released in the late 1950s and early 1960s. Coates has also talked about how her editing supports and enhances film actors' performances. Her editing of sequences involving the protagonists in *Tunes of Glory*, and Lawrence and Ali in *Lawrence*, helped to bring out subtleties within the emotional relationships between these male characters (see Genre: The male epic).

Coates's work as *Lawrence*'s editor won her an Oscar. Working closely with Lean on the editing of this epic proved to be a turning-point in her career. It led to subsequent work with directors as diverse as David Lynch and Richard Attenborough. Coates, along with other members of the original production team, was involved in the restoration of *Lawrence* which preceded the film's rerelease in 1989 (see Production history: Reediting and restoration). She continues to work on a variety of projects. Two notable recent films Coates edited were *In the Line of Fire* (Wolfgang Petersen, 1993) and *Out of Sight* (Steven Soderbergh, 1998).

director as auteur

Studying a director as an 'auteur' involves looking for thematic and stylistic consistencies and developments across the entire body of that director's work. The auteur approach is one amongst several which can be adopted when analysing films. One problem with it is that it can minimise the contributions made by other people working on the film. The biographies of key players outlined above counterbalance this by highlighting some of skills and experience other contributors brought to *Lawrence of Arabia*. Lean himself always sought out the best collaborators available to help him realise his film projects.

The auteur approach is not sufficient in itself because it also tends to ignore the fact that many audiences are drawn towards, understand, and enjoy films for reasons which have little to do with their directors (see Audience). Genre and stars are equally if not more important factors. Many audiences approach *Lawrence* primarily as an epic film. They are likely to watch it because they are fans of that genre, and not necessarily because they wish to understand it as a David Lean film (see Filmography, and Genre: The male epic). Similarly, the stars in *Lawrence* enable audiences to relate to the film in particular ways (see Production history: Casting). Nevertheless, the auteur approach is one amongst several which can be used to analyse *Lawrence*. Combined with other methods of analysis, it can yield some useful insights.

The idea of identifying the directors of certain films as auteurs is most famously associated with the critics writing for the French magazine *Cahiers du Cinéma* in the 1950s. Many of these critics reacted forcefully against the respectful literary adaptations common within French cinema at this time. These critics were particularly concerned to identify as auteurs Hollywood directors who had previously received little serious critical attention. The most controversial aspect of the *Cahiers* critics' approach was their argument that some Hollywood directors hitherto seen as competent, efficient technicians were in fact profoundly serious artists with distinctive worldviews and identifiably personal themes and styles. Similar approaches were gradually developed by critics elsewhere. Andrew Sarris pioneered auteurisme in America, and the writers associated with *Movie* magazine promoted it in Britain (see Cultural Contexts: Critical responses).

David Lean was never celebrated in the 1950s or 1960s by leading auteurist critics. His films were praised by mainstream newspaper reviewers like Dilys Powell and Alexander Walker for their technical excellence, but Lean was not seen as a director with a distinctive personal vision. Auteurist critics such as Andrew Sarris and the *Cahiers* and *Movie* writers tended to focus on American rather than British directors. Lean was suspect, from their point of view, because many of his films appealed to conventional good taste by being adaptations of prestigious literary works. Many auteurist critics in the 1950s and 1960s preferred directors who wrote their own scripts or who based their films upon pulp fiction rather than respectable authors like Noël Coward, Charles Dickens and Boris Pasternak. Avoiding classic literature seemed to allow more scope for an auteur's own personal vision to emerge.

Lean was not a director favoured by the first wave of auteurist critics. However, auteurisme became so prevalent that eventually some critics did reassess his films from this perspective. In the mid-1970s Gerald Pratley published a book on Lean which noted persistent themes running throughout his films. Pratley argues that class, and the way it shapes individual attitudes, was a consistent preoccupation within Lean's work. This is evident in films like *Brief Encounter*, where the passion the two protagonists feel for each other clashes with their middle-class values. *Lawrence* hints in one sequence that Lawrence's insecurity about his family background, class and social status is one of the factors motivating this enigmatic character (see Ideology: Marginality and romantic orientalism). Certainly issues of class are relevant to Lean's work, but this is a preoccupation which runs through many other British directors' work as well.

Pratley also notes that unhappy, unfulfilled or unacknowledged love affairs are another constant in Lean's films. Once again, *Brief Encounter* is the best example here. The passion the protagonists feel for each other is never consummated. Other examples of frustrated love affairs occur in *Summertime* (1955), *Ryan's Daughter* (1970), and many other Lean films.

director as auteur background

The poignant, compelling emotional relationship between Lawrence and Sherif Ali in *Lawrence* could be related to this persistent theme in Lean's work (see Genre: The male epic). Michael Anderegg, who published an auteurist study of Lean's films in the 1980s, discusses their obliquely powerful representation of emotion and sexual desire, especially in *Lawrence*. This approach to the representation of emotion and sexual desire can also be seen as characteristic of many British films made during the 1940s, 1950s and 1960s.

Pratley observes that another constant throughout many Lean films is characters who indulge in romanticisation and get lost in their own subjective views of the world. Colonel Nicholson, the central figure in *Kwai*, is an officer leading a group of British prisoners in a Japanese prisoner of war camp in Burma. He is determined to demonstrate British technological excellence and superior self-discipline to the Japanese. He drives his men mercilessly to complete a bridge the Japanese commander Colonel Saito has ordered them to build. Nicholson is so determined to prove his point that he ignores the fact that what he is doing is helping the Japanese war effort. *Lawrence* features an equally driven, obsessive protagonist who tries to impose his vision upon the world. Lawrence is an even more complex character than Nicholson because he is also prone to self-doubt.

Anderegg analyses set design, mise-en-scène and cinematography in Lean's films in more detail than Pratley does. These stylistic features are crucially important in *Lawrence* (see Cinematography and mise-en-scène). Anderegg points out that Lean's Dickens adaptations attempt to project subjective realities onto the objective world. *Oliver Twist*'s London, for example, is represented as dark, distorted and menacing, reflecting the characters' fears and feelings.

In *Brief Encounter* Laura's subjectivity is often mirrored in the representation of the world around her. For example, as Laura travels on a train she looks out of a window. Romantic images of her and Alec, the married man she is falling in love with, are projected onto the window. Laura and Alec part at the end of the film. Lighting dims around a close-up of Laura's face, and camera movement creates a canted framing. Subsequent shots of Laura running in distress to the edge of the platform representation unrealistic?

are also canted. The representation of the environment in *Brief Encounter* never becomes entirely unrealistic, yet it clearly reflects the central protagonists' feelings. *Lawrence*, through the combined efforts of Lean, cinematographer Freddie Young, designer John Box, and other production workers, achieves similar effects (see Realism, exoticism, and subjectivity).

narrative & form

Lawrence of Arabia's narrative drive and complexity derive in large part from its excellent script, cinematography and editing. Without departing too radically from classical Hollywood conventions, the film achieves a number of sophisticated narrative effects (see Hollywood narratives). It constructs Lawrence as a goal-orientated, but nevertheless relatively enigmatic protagonist. It employs various narrative devices in order to raise, but not conclusively answer, questions about Lawrence's historical significance and legendary status (see Hollywood narratives: Character and history, and Narrative circularity). Finally, the complexity of the narrative and development of characters within it can be related to a set of conventional assumptions regarding England and Arabia, and the West and the East. On one level the narrative reiterates these assumptions. On other more subtle levels it questions them (see Non-linear structures, Ideology: Orientalism, and Ideology: Ambivalence).

hollywood narratives

Lawrence of Arabia conforms to many of the general principles of classical Hollywood narrative. These are discussed in detail in David Bordwell, Janet Staiger and Kristin Thompson, *The Classical Hollywood Cinema*. In the broadest terms the film's narrative can be broken down into the five conventional sections of *exposition, conflict, complication, crisis*, and *dénouement*. Many Hollywood films follow this pattern. Each section is linked to the others by chains of cause and effect which are primarily character-centred. Lawrence's psychology and actions drive much of the first part of the narrative. Other characters' motivations play an increasingly prominent role within the cause and effect chain which unfolds in the latter part of the narrative.

Within classical Hollywood narratives the *expository* section is where protagonists' distinctive character traits, motivations and goals are outlined. In *Lawrence*'s *expository* section, Lawrence's manner of speaking and physical bearing mark him out as different from other British officers stationed in Cairo during the First World War. Britain is at war with Turkey in the Middle East and Lawrence follows reports of Bedouin attacks upon Turkish outposts with interest. The diplomat Dryden recommends that Lawrence is dispatched into the desert to make an assessment of the Arab Prince Feisal's campaign against the Turks. Lawrence's first encounter with Sherif Ali takes place when Ali shoots his guide Tafas at the Masturah well. Ali explains that he is a member of the Harith Bedouin tribe. Tafas is from another tribe, the Beni Salem, who are not allowed to drink at wells in Harith territory. In a passionately delivered piece of dialogue, Lawrence articulates his ambitious historical goal as Ali rides away:

Lawrence (calling after him)

> Sherif Ali! So long as the Arabs fight tribe against tribe, so long will they be a little people.

107 Close up. Lawrence, emphasizing every word.

Lawrence

> A silly people! Greedy, barbarous, and cruel — as you are!

Lawrence's ultimate historical objective, it becomes clear, is to unite the Arabs and help to make them great again. The next section of the narrative works through some of the *conflict* this involves. When Lawrence arrives at Prince Feisal's camp two Turkish aeroplanes are strafing Feisal's army. From this point onwards, however, Turkish forces are not the only obstacle which needs to be overcome. The British military establishment, represented within Feisal's camp by Colonel Brighton, has to be convinced of the seriousness of the incipient Arab revolt. Unity between Arabs also has to be achieved. Lawrence crosses the Nefud desert with Sherif Ali and some of Feisal's men. He brings Auda Abu Tayi and his Howeitat tribe into the Arab coalition. The united Arab army inflicts its first serious defeat on the Turks at Aqaba.

In the next major section, and in the latter part of the narrative, *complication* ensues. On the journey back to Cairo to report Aqaba's capture Daud, Lawrence's Bedouin companion, dies in quicksand. Lawrence starts to exhibit signs of exhaustion, guilt, and trauma. The British General Allenby's and the politician Dryden's imperial ambitions with regard to Arabia become increasingly clear to the film's spectator. Back in Arabia, Lawrence is temporarily detained in Deraa and subjected to sexual violence by the Turkish bey there.

When Lawrence returns to British military headquarters in Jerusalem he expresses a wish not to return to the desert, but is nevertheless persuaded by Allenby to do so. Lawrence's and the Arab army's part in the campaign to capture Damascus becomes increasingly bloodthirsty and ruthless. It is made more urgent by a deadline. This is typical classical Hollywood narrative device, used to focus attention on characters' goals and heighten anticipation for the resolution of the narrative. Lawrence aims to arrive in Damascus before Allenby does, so that the city can be governed by the Arabs rather than the British army.

Crisis point is reached when the Arab army arrives in Damascus. Despite Lawrence's best efforts the Arabs prove incapable of governing the city. *Dénouement* takes place as a result of compromises reached behind closed doors between the British generals and politicians and Prince Feisal. In the film's penultimate sequence Allenby, Dryden, and Feisal haggle over the allocation of power and territory within the newly liberated Middle East. Feisal drives a hard bargain but settles for less than full political independence. Lawrence slips out of the room and silently returns to England.

INTERDEPENDENT LINES OF ACTION

Another narrative convention of classical Hollywood cinema relevant to *Lawrence of Arabia* is the intertwining of lines of action. In most cases at least one of these lines of action involves heterosexual romantic love. Typically, Hollywood epics of the 1950s and 1960s entwine a romantic line of action with one dealing with momentous developments in world history (see Filmography). *Lawrence of Arabia* does not include heterosexual romance as one of its lines of action, although it can be argued that the relationship between Lawrence and Sherif Ali implicitly fulfils this function (see Genre: The male epic).

The two most prominent lines of action in *Lawrence* are motivated, on the one hand, by Lawrence's personal desire to escape from routine, to transform himself by going into the desert, and to do unusual things (see Ideology: Marginality and romantic orientalism). The other main line of action is motivated by various individuals' attempts to influence the course of history. Lawrence is the one character who is central to both lines of action, but each line also has its own separate logic.

Lawrence's first dialogue exchange in the narrative is with a fellow soldier also working in a basement room making maps in Cairo. It immediately establishes Lawrence's desire for escape, and difference from the people around him, by demonstrating one of his unusual character traits. Lawrence looks up to see a camel passing in the street, and says:

```
Lawrence (gloomily)
        Michael George Hartley, this is a nasty, dark
        little room.
Sergeant
        'T's right.
Lawrence
        We are not happy in it.
Sergeant (thinking of the trenches)
        I am.
Lawrence
        Then you are an ignoble fellow.
Sergeant
        'T's right.
```

Another soldier arrives, lights a cigarette, and Lawrence extinguishes the match with his bare hand. This hints at Lawrence's ability or even sadomasochistic desire to endure and inflict pain. Twice the other soldiers refer to Lawrence as 'barmy'. Later, in a conversation with Dryden just before his first journey to the desert, Lawrence expands on some of his personal motivations for wishing to go to there:

```
Lawrence throws back his head in silent rapture.
Lawrence
        Oh thanks, Dryden, this is going to be fun!
Dryden
                Lawrence, only two types of creature get 'fun'
                in the desert, Bedouins  and - (his gaze
                wanders round the photographs of silent sun-
                scorched figures and the fragments of stone) -
                gods. And you're neither. Take it from me for
                ordinary men it's a burning fiery furnace.
Lawrence (very quietly)
                No, Dryden, it's going to be fun.
The set intensity of his expression is in utter
contradiction to his words.
Close up. Dryden. He looks from the burning match in
Lawrence's fingers to Lawrence's face.
Dryden (rather sourly)
                It is recognized that you have a funny sense
                of fun.
```

Lawrence's desire for 'fun' and adventure is specifically related at the beginning of the narrative to a compulsion to put himself in perilous or painful situations (see Genre: The male epic). These situations include his rescue of the Bedouin Gasim when he gets lost crossing the Nefud, and particularly his encounter with the Turkish bey in Deraa. Lawrence's desire to transform himself into something other than an Englishman is also established in the narrative's expository section. On his first desert journey within the film his Bedu guide Tafas offers him water but he refuses to drink until Tafas does. As far as is possible, Lawrence wants to escape from his national identity and blur the distinction between himself and the Bedouin.

CHARACTER AND HISTORY

Lawrence's personal qualities and motivations have larger ramifications for the narrative's second major line of action; influence over the course of history. They enable him to unite the Arabs and capture Aqaba. However, Lawrence is not the only character in the film who seeks to influence the course of history. By the time that the narrative reaches its dénouement, Dryden's motivation for dispatching Lawrence to Arabia becomes retrospectively apparent. He wishes to extend British control over the Middle East. In the latter part of the narrative Allenby, Dryden, and to a lesser extent Feisal assume an increasingly prominent role in causing historical events to happen. For example in Damascus Allenby confines British troops, especially technical and medical staff, to barracks. He does this in order to undermine the Arab national council's attempt to govern the city.

The relationship between character and history in *Lawrence of Arabia* conforms to the broad conventions of the Hollywood historical epic insofar as significant individuals drive history forward. The actions of important individuals, such as leaders, men of destiny, or ordinary mortals accidentally caught up in historical events, are represented as decisive within the narrative chain of cause and effect. Longer-term, non-individual economic, social, and political processes are rarely dramatised or analysed in any depth.

narrative circularity

Lawrence of Arabia's opening sequence foregrounds Lawrence as an enigma (see Production history: Casting). In this sequence Lawrence mounts a motorcycle as the credits roll, speeds some distance along an English country lane, swerves to avoid two cyclists, is thrown from his bike, and dies. The first shot in the film is from a high overhead position which makes it impossible for the spectator to see Lawrence's face. The next shot is from behind Lawrence's legs as he climbs onto his motorcycle. Camera movement opens the frame up into a long shot of Lawrence driving away down a country lane. Subsequent moving camera shots reveal his face, but his eyes remain obscured by motorcycling goggles. Throughout this sequence Lawrence says nothing. Narration here gives the spectator minimal access to Lawrence's psychology.

The next sequence in the narrative takes place immediately after Lawrence's funeral service in St Paul's cathedral. Various characters who reappear later in the plot, but earlier in the actual chronological story, comment on Lawrence. These include Colonel Brighton and Lord, previously General, Allenby. Most confess they didn't really know him. The only person who says he knew him well is Jackson Bentley. He is the American journalist responsible for publicising and perhaps exaggerating Lawrence's exploits (see Self-conscious romanticisation). Characters' opinions in this sequence are divided about Lawrence's true character and the extent of his historical significance. The narrative then shifts back in time to Cairo during the First World War.

The American film trade magazine *Variety* judges new film releases according to their accessibility and potential appeal to audiences used to classical Hollywood conventions. *Variety*'s reviewer found the jump forward in time at the beginning of *Lawrence* confusing. It is relatively unusual for an epic film, but it serves to raise questions about Lawrence's personality and the nature of his achievements. These questions grow in intensity during the latter part of the narrative, after the capture of Aqaba. Questions about Lawrence's character and motivations are never entirely resolved. This can cause some confusion and dissatisfaction for spectators expecting a more conventional classical Hollywood narrative resolution. Usually, there is more of an attempt to tie loose threads together and answer outstanding questions.

Variety's reviewer correctly highlighted the way that *Lawrence*'s narrative does in certain respects deviate from the norms of classical Hollywood. These deviations can be seen as a fault, or they can be seen as widening the range of interpretations which can plausibly be derived from the film (see Character transformations, Ideology: Ambivalence, and Genre: The male epic). *Lawrence*'s narrative builds a sense of complexity and intriguing contradictions around its protagonist. As British film critic Penelope Gilliat wrote of Lawrence's character in the film, 'there seem to be at least ten incompatible men living under the same skin, and two or three women as well'.

Lawrence's identity is put into question as the latter part of the narrative progresses. The first person Lawrence encounters on arriving back in Egypt after the capture of Aqaba is a soldier on a motorcycle. He calls out from a distance 'Who are you?' Lawrence does not respond. The motorcyclist recalls Lawrence's own motorcycle ride in the opening sequence. He poses a question which neither Lawrence nor the spectator can answer. In the film's closing shots Lawrence leaves Cairo for England. As in the opening sequence, his face is again obscured, this time by the dirty windshield of the car he is travelling in. Lawrence observes another motorcycle rider overtaking his car. Caught between England and Arabia, belonging by the end of the narrative to neither, Lawrence sees a portent of his own death.

Lawrence of Arabia's ending rhymes with its beginning. It gives the narrative a sense of formal closure. The ending also reiterates questions posed earlier in the narrative about whether Lawrence has really achieved anything substantial (see Hollywood narratives: Character and history, and Self-conscious romanticisation). Ending with the motorcycle rider and with a trip back to England, where the narrative began, creates an impression of circularity rather than linearity. In other words the narrative, on one level, doubles back on itself rather than progressing along a straight line towards a clear goal. The circular narrative structure and lack of clear resolution at the end leave some questions unanswered. Have Lawrence's adventures in the desert achieved anything? Have they taken him anywhere except back to where he started from?

restricted and unrestricted narration

Another narrative process encourages further questions on the spectator's part regarding Lawrence's historical significance. This is the gradual shift from restricted to unrestricted narration. This shift gathers pace in the latter part of the narrative after the capture of Aqaba. Up to that point in the narrative most sequences feature Lawrence quite prominently. The range of what the spectator knows is broadly restricted to Lawrence's range of knowledge. The causal chains represented within this part of the narrative tend to have Lawrence at their centre. Lawrence succeeds in finding Prince Feisal, crossing the Nefud, uniting the Arabs, and capturing Aqaba. His centrality within these lines of action contributes to the generally heroic and optimistic tone of this first part of the narrative.

By the end of the narrative, the range of the spectator's knowledge exceeds Lawrence's. Unrestricted narration moves between sequences involving Lawrence and the Arab army to sequences involving Allenby and Dryden, Feisal and Jackson Bentley, or Auda Abu Tayi and Sherif Ali separate from Lawrence. Lawrence is still an important narrative agent but unrestricted narration places him as one amongst several narrative agents. Lawrence does not know about and is not in control of everything that happens in the narrative. He becomes a character events happen to as well as one who makes events happen. This contributes to the gloomier, desolate tone of the latter part of the narrative. It provides a context for Lawrence's increasingly evident despair and disillusionment.

self-conscious romanticisation

Immediately after Lawrence has returned to the desert from Cairo, approximately half way through the narrative, there is a short sequence in which the American journalist Jackson Bentley meets Prince Feisal. Bentley is the last major protagonist to be introduced into the narrative. He is a crucial factor in the gradual change of tone within its latter part. Feisal and

Bentley agree that they have common interests. Bentley is looking for a good story. Feisal wants the story of the Arab revolt to be told. Bentley explains that he is looking for a romantic hero and an adventurous narrative for American newspaper readers. He feels that this will help to build support for America entering the war. Lawrence is the obvious candidate. From this point onwards Bentley follows Lawrence's campaign, photographing and writing about his exploits.

Bentley is with Lawrence during much of the latter part of narrative, constantly taking dramatic photographs, which Lawrence often poses for. Once again this highlights questions about Lawrence's identity and historical significance. In the St Paul's cathedral sequence, Bentley is the only person who claims to have truly known Lawrence. However, he is the character most responsible for turning Lawrence into a legend. Whilst Bentley is turning him into a legend, Lawrence becomes increasingly traumatised by the violence and bloodshed of the campaign. Yet Lawrence often seems so caught up in this violence and bloodshed, and in his own legend, that he seems unable to stop. These factors within the narrative make it difficult for spectators to arrive at conclusive judgements about Lawrence's personality, personal motivations and actual historical significance.

Lawrence of Arabia's narrative opens up the question of whether Lawrence was an extraordinary man or whether he was an ordinary one trapped within the legend of his own extraordinariness. In the earlier part of the narrative Lawrence certainly aspires to be extraordinary and to make history happen through his own volition. When crossing the Nefud desert Gasim, one of the camel riders, gets lost. The other Arabs in the caravan accept this fatalistically. One says 'Gasim's time is come, Aurens [the Arabs' name for Laurence] … It is written.' Yet Lawrence goes back and rescues Gasim, returning to tell Sherif Ali '*Nothing* is written.' Later, after the campaign against the Turks suffers some setbacks, Sherif Ali asks Lawrence to set the irregular Arab army more realistic targets:

```
Unwittingly, Ali has challenged him at the mingled
root of his strength and weakness and must now face
Lawrence's whole personality up in arms.
```

romanticisation narrative & form

Lawrence

> Who are you to know what can be done? If we'd
> done what you thought could be done we'd be
> back in 'Yenbo now, and nowhere!
>
> Whatever I ask them to be done can be done,
> that's all ... they know that if you don't
> ...!

He drops the cloth, backing from Ali towards a
broken opening in the interior wall.

Lawrence (cont)

> ... D' you think I'm just anybody, Ali? Do
> you?

Before Ali can reply, he turns from him towards
the opening and calls in a voice ostensibly warm
and confident with an unconscious undernote of
fear:

> My friends, who will walk on water with me?

At this point Lawrence seems to suggest that, given self-belief and the
belief of others, the impossible can be achieved.

After his encounter with the Turkish bey in Deraa, Lawrence expresses
for the first time a desire to leave the desert and be ordinary again. Ali
turns Lawrence's earlier arguments back on him. He reminds Lawrence
that '"A man can be whatever he wants." You said'. Later in the narrative
Allenby tries a similar ploy when Lawrence wavers over whether to return
to the desert and continue to lead the Arab revolt. The latter part of
Lawrence's narrative sets up a tension between the ordinary and the
extraordinary and between history and legend. It blurs the distinction
between them. It shows how Lawrence's legend is itself a historical factor.
Within the narrative it becomes something which mobilises Ali and the
Arabs and generates much interest and enthusiasm through Bentley's
reporting. The making of the film itself, more than forty years after the
desert campaign, testifies to the legend's continuing appeal (see Ideology:
Orientalism).

Lawrence and Bentley

non-linear structures

STRUCTURALISM AND BINARY OPPOSITIONS

Structuralism is a critical approach which can help in analysing *Lawrence of Arabia*'s narrative. As a practical method of analysis it can yield some useful basic insights into certain films. The anthropologist Claude Lévi-Strauss was one of the pioneers of structuralism. His analysis of myths in ancient and so-called primitive societies has been influential in film studies. The first step in Lévi-Strauss's approach involves identifying the binary oppositions which structure a myth or a set of myths. This method of analysis is non-linear because, in the first instance, it is not especially concerned with the order in which these elements occur within the narrative. What it is concerned with is highlighting the underlying structural oppositions which recur throughout particular narratives.

The function of myth, Lévi-Strauss argued, was to symbolically resolve or work through oppositions and contradictions which exist within the culture the myth belongs to. Myth does not *logically* resolve these oppositions and contradictions. It resolves them within a narrative audiences find satisfying because its structure brings them together. Binary oppositions in *Lawrence of Arabia* would include the following:

- culture/nature
- the city/the desert
- West/East
- European/Arab
- civilisation/barbarism
- compassion/violence
- drab/exotic

Many elements within *Lawrence of Arabia*'s narrative could be arranged under these two columns, and other pairs of binary oppositions could be identified. Space is just one element within the narrative which can be subjected to structuralist analysis. Analysing the organisation of space within the narrative in relation to the binary oppositions set out above will demonstrate the type of insights which can be generated by a structuralist approach.

SPACE

Graeme Turner, in his discussion of structuralist analysis of film narratives in Chapter Four of *Film as Social Practice*, distinguishes between narratives where binary oppositions are apparently resolved and narratives where one side of the opposition eventually takes precedence over the other. *Lawrence of Arabia* does neither. Characters such as Lawrence and to a lesser extent Ali try to mediate oppositions between opposing terms, but to a significant degree these opposing terms remain in place at the end of the narrative. This becomes clear through an analysis how space is organised within the film.

Throughout the narrative there is a definite opposition between two types of space, the city and the desert. The contrast is best exemplified by the famous cut from a close-up of Lawrence blowing out a lighted match in a room in the British military headquarters in Cairo to an extreme long shot of the sun slowly rising over a desert horizon (see Editing: Transitions between sequences). These shots demonstrate another of the basic oppositions associated with the city/desert pair. This is an opposition between confined, interior space and expansive, exterior locations. The former is primarily the domain of Europeans, the latter of Arabs.

Certain characters in *Lawrence of Arabia* remain exclusively associated throughout the narrative with one side of the narrative's spatial opposition. General Allenby and Dryden are always represented within cities, interior space, or near monumental urban architecture. Auda Abu Tayi is primarily associated with the desert and his final act in the narrative is to return there. Cities are associated with civilisation, politics, and manipulative imperial strategies. The desert is a space of both freedom and exotic beauty as well as violence and barbarism. Lawrence refers to the desert as a 'clean' place, compared to the city, and for much of the film it is represented as amazingly beautiful (see Cinematography and mise-en-scène). Yet the desert is also where Lawrence witnesses and participates in some of the most extreme acts of violence shown in the film.

Farraj in the officers' bar

Lawrence and Farraj
return to Cairo

LAWRENCE OF ARABIA

Lawrence, unlike Allenby and Dryden and Auda Abu Tayi, can be seen as a protagonist who attempts to mediate between two types of space, the city and the desert. From a structuralist perspective certain points within the narrative can be seen as moments when binary oppositions are brought together but not successfully reconciled. Two sequences in particular illustrate this. The first occurs approximately half way through the narrative when Lawrence returns with Farraj from the desert to report to the senior British officers in Cairo that he and the Arabs have captured Aqaba. The second is towards the end of the narrative when Damascus has been captured and the Arab national council meet to attempt to organise the city's governance.

When Lawrence and Farraj arrive in Cairo Lawrence is still dressed in his Arab robes. They walk up steps into the grand, columned building which is the British military headquarters. Despite challenges by soldiers on guard duty, they walk on to the officers' bar. This is the same location in which Lawrence, at the beginning of the narrative, bumped into other officers and appeared distinctly ill at ease. This time he makes a dramatic entrance. Conversation falls silent as Lawrence and Farraj walk through the room. The barkeeper refuses to serve them and an officer tries to eject Farraj. When Lawrence announces the capture of Aqaba, hostility is transformed into amazement and Brighton agrees to find a bed for Farraj:

Brighton

    Taken Akaba? Who has?

Lawrence

    We have ... Our side in the war has. The wogs
    have. We have.

In this sequence, and especially in Lawrence's deliberate conflation of 'our side' and the 'wogs', there is a temporary reconciliation of oppositions. After initial resistance Farraj, and Lawrence in his Arab robes, are accepted into European space. Farraj, a Bedouin boy from the desert, gets to sleep in a bed in the city for the first time in his life. The news of Aqaba's capture suggests that the Arabs can be an organised and disciplined rather than

Lawrence and Auda Abu Tayi
at the chaotic meeting of the
Arab national council in Damascus

anarchic and barbarous military force. Even in this sequence, however, the oppositions are not entirely reconciled. Lawrence trembles as he drinks his lemonade at the bar whilst recalling the excessive amount of bloodshed involved in taking Aqaba. The memory of the first time in the film that Arabs have entered city space disturbs Lawrence.

The second sequence in *Lawrence of Arabia* which brings desert Arabs and the values associated with them into city space occurs in Damascus towards the end of the narrative. The meeting of the Arab national council takes place inside a vast chamber in a grand city building. Hordes of Bedouin inside generate an overwhelming cacophony, drowning out individual dialogue until Lawrence bangs on a table to bring order to the meeting. His attempt to get different factions to supervise vital services such as the city electricity supply and telephone exchange ends in failure. Chaos predominates and the Bedouin soon leave the city.

From a structuralist perspective, *Lawrence* suggests that the city and the desert, and all of the other oppositions associated with them, are fundamentally irreconcilable. Auda Abu Tayi asks Lawrence to return to the desert with him. Sherif Ali decides to stay in the city and 'learn politics', but Auda Abu Tayi's last warning to him, after they clash outside the council chamber, is that this will not be as easy as he thinks.

Lawrence does not take up Auda Abu Tayi's invitation to return to the desert, but neither does he belong to European city space. By the end of the narrative there is literally no place left for him within the film's spatial oppositions. In the final sequence Lawrence returns to England. The only information *Lawrence's* narrative supplies about his life there, in the opening sequence, is that this is where he will die. According to structuralist theory, conventional mythic narratives satisfactorily resolve binary oppositions. *Lawrence of Arabia* does not do this (see Ideology: Orientalism). From a structuralist perspective, Lawrence's tragedy is to have tried and failed to reconcile the binary oppositions underlying the film's narrative.

LIMITATIONS OF STRUCTURALISM

Structuralist analysis can produce some useful insights into film narratives. However, one criticism of this approach is that, although it may be adequate for the analysis of myths in ancient and so-called primitive societies, it is not equipped to deal with the more subtle nuances of narration in complex film texts. Lévi-Strauss searched for the common factors within different versions of the same myth circulating within a culture. Moreover, myths are narratives without authors. *Lawrence of Arabia* is by contrast a unique text produced by sophisticated collaborators such as David Lean, Robert Bolt and Michael Wilson.

In *Lawrence* it could be argued that the civilisation/barbarism opposition is complicated by the crosscutting between the Arab national council meeting in Damascus and Allenby's attempts to undermine it by confining technical and medical staff to barracks (see Restricted and unrestricted narration). Allenby manipulates the situation to ensure that the Arabs live up to expectations. Similarly, the narrative constructs Lawrence as an enigmatic character whose motivations and actions are open to different interpretations (see Narrative circularity). This allows for the possibility that Lawrence's violent and extreme encounters in the desert are partly a projection of his own desires rather than stemming from innate Arab characteristics (see Realism, exoticism, and subjectivity, and Ideology: Ambivalence).

Steven Caton in his book on *Lawrence* identifies several moments within the narrative which potentially undermine the basic binary oppositions outlined above. For example, he points out that Lawrence's comment to Ali at the Masturah well about Arabs being 'barbarous and cruel' can be seen as deeply ironic. The overarching historical context for the film is the First World War, where millions of soldiers were slaughtered by 'advanced' technology on European battlefields. Later, as the Arab army progresses towards Damascus, Lawrence and Ali observe a distant British artillery bombardment of Turkish troops. Ali whispers 'God help the men who lie under that'. There are a number of points in the narrative when associations of barbarism and violence are removed from the Arabs and the desert and attached to the ostensibly civilised British.

character
transformations

The relationship between Lawrence and Ali is central to *Lawrence of Arabia*'s narrative in several respects (see Realism, exoticism and subjectivity, and Genre: The male epic). As the narrative develops, Lawrence exemplifies some of the qualities initially associated with Ali, and vice versa. This process of doubling, transference, and transformation proves to be problematic for both characters. The effect which Lawrence's interaction with Ali, the Arabs, and the desert has on his personality adds to his enigma and complexity. It constitutes one of the key points of narrative interest.

Lawrence, attracted to the exotic beauty, 'fun' and adventure he expects to find in the desert, also brings with him to the desert what at first seems to be the primarily European value of compassion. In their first encounter at the Masturah well, Lawrence is appalled by Ali's apparently nonchalant attitude towards killing his guide Tafas. Rescuing Gasim during their crossing of the Nefud desert provides a lesson in compassion for Ali. It graphically demonstrates Lawrence's belief that 'nothing is written', as well as possibly being his way of atoning for guilt over being involved in Tafas's death.

Lawrence's first ethical crisis within the narrative occurs after Ali's and Auda Abu Tayi's tribes have agreed to unite for the purpose of capturing Aqaba. A member of Ali's Harith tribe kills one of Auda's Howeitat men in a quarrel. Lawrence offers to carry out the punishment in order to prevent disunity through further blood feuding. The man he must kill is Gasim, whose identity is only revealed to Lawrence a moment before the execution. This is the first indication of how, in the quest to achieve his narrative goal, Lawrence becomes thoroughly immersed in the harshness and violence which seem to permeate desert life in the film.

Lawrence's companion Daud dies in desert quicksand during the first journey back to Cairo. As well as a natural disaster, this can also be seen as a fatal consequence, for someone else, of Lawrence's sadomasochistic desire to experience pain and push himself and other people beyond the limits of human endurance. Lawrence is pale, stunned, and speechless for some time after this. Later he has to kill his other companion, Farraj. Farraj is wounded by a detonator, and killing him is preferable to leaving him to be tortured by the Turks. The last battle before the Arab army reaches Damascus involves an attack upon a straggling Turkish platoon who have just razed a Bedouin village, killing all the inhabitants. One of Lawrence's men, who is from this village, charges ahead and is shot down by retreating Turks. A high angle shot of his body lying on bloodstained desert sand echoes the first shot of a dead body in the film – Tafas after he has been killed by Ali at the Masturah well. Trembling, agitated, Lawrence orders and participates in a bloody massacre of Turks in which no prisoners are taken.

Lawrence's belief in Arab unity and his earlier acts of compassion fail to change what the film on one level represents as qualities and values inherent within desert existence. The desert as represented in the film has appealing qualities, such as a chance to escape from routine, from the English identity Lawrence finds so restricting, and beautiful exoticism (see Cinematography and mise-en-scène). Yet it is also linked to negative qualities, to a cycle of blood, violence, strife, and death. Lawrence's attempt to introduce compassion and political unity into the desert fails, but the desert succeeds in bringing out some of the elements of harshness and violence within his character.

The desert can be seen as providing Lawrence with a stage for playing out some of the sadomasochistic aspects of his character hinted at in the narrative's expository section (see Hollywood narratives). Lawrence's desire to transform himself into something other than an Englishman propels him into extreme situations and confrontations with himself which he finds difficult to deal with. By the end of the film Lawrence is a silent, diminished figure stranded between the two different worlds of England and Arabia.

As the narrative progresses Ali's character transforms in an opposite direction to Lawrence's. He gradually softens and takes on some of the compassionate traits and political aspirations which were at first primarily associated with Lawrence. After the final massacre of the Turkish platoon, Ali bitterly and ironically turns the comment about being 'barbarous and cruel' back onto Lawrence. Yet Ali's final action within the narrative is ambiguous. It could be understood as implying that this transformation might be relatively superficial. Ali clashes with Auda, who mocks his recently acquired political commitment to Arab unity. Ali reaches for his sword, cursing Auda and his Howeitat tribe. This is reminiscent of Ali's first action within the narrative which involved killing a Bedu from another tribe for trespassing on his well.

Ali's final action opens up the question of how far he has travelled from his initial position. To a certain extent his progression through the narrative is, like Lawrence's, a circular one which returns him back to where he started. However, there are differences as well as similarities between the first and last sequences Ali appears in. He clashes with Auda but, unlike the earlier encounter with Tafas at the Masturah well, doesn't kill his adversary from another tribe. Ali is resolved to pursue a political career, and the narrative leaves open the possibility that he might attain his objectives. Ali as played by Omar Sharif is certainly one of the most complex Arab characters represented in a Hollywood film. Of all the characters Ali comes closest to moving beyond the binary oppositions underlying the film's narrative.

style

cinematography & mise-en-scène

Visual style in *Lawrence of Arabia* contributes to the flow of the narrative and adds levels of meaning and affect to the film. Freddie Young's widescreen cinematography is one of the main factors regulating the difference in tone between the two halves of the narrative before and after the capture of Aqaba. Cinematography works in conjunction with the mise-en-scène. Mise-en-scène is a French term, derived from the theatre, meaning 'having been put into the scene'. In film it involves the organisation of elements such as location, props, and actors within the shot. If the camera moves this must also be taken into consideration. Throughout the film cinematography and mise-en-scène are carefully coordinated to further the narrative and produce particular visual effects.

One example of how these stylistic elements work together is Lawrence's first desert journey with Tafas to the Masturah well. This is filmed in a brilliant, warm, predominantly orange hue. Their progress is represented through a series of sometimes extreme long shots. As they travel slow camera movements follow their movements and add further depth to the images as new dimensions of the desert landscape are revealed. In this first journey Lawrence becomes an increasingly confident camel rider. The final image of him and Tafas speeding across the desert prior to their arrival at the well is a crane shot. Specifically, it is a rapidly moving long shot taken from a helicopter. Colour, framing, and camera movement all contribute to the exhilarating tone of this sequence.

Cinematography and mise-en-scène in the first part of the narrative produce a variety of tones according to the particular landscape and situation. The overarching tone up to the capture of Aqaba is one of dynamism and exuberance. The Nefud desert is the first major obstacle to be overcome. It is flatter and bleaker than the first stretch of desert Lawrence and Tafas cross, and is predominantly shot in ominous, subdued dark blue tones. However, Lawrence's party cross it successfully and he rescues Gasim. Immediately after this, Lawrence dons Arab robes for the first time against the now cool yellow of the desert sand and a clear blue sky (see Costume). When Auda Abu Tayi's Howeitat tribe join the Arab revolt, the cinematography moves into a sustained series of extreme long shots. These encompass an army of extras riding horses and camels and bearing colourful flags. This important moment of Arab unity is highlighted through visual spectacle.

As this Arab army leaves Wadi Rhumm to head for Aqaba, exceptionally spectacular shot compositions feature a group of women in the foreground, the entire army in the middle distance, and imposing mountains in the background. These static compositions utilise the potential of the widescreen format to create an incredible sense of depth. The attack on Aqaba demonstrates the dynamic effects that camera movements in this format can create. Arab riders charge from screen left to screen right in a series of tracking shots taken from different angles and distances from the action. These culminate in an extreme high angle left to right panning shot lasting over forty seconds. In this shot Arab riders surge through the conquered city. The camera movement ends with a Turkish gun emplacement in the foreground, facing towards the sea rather than the desert from which the Arabs have unexpectedly emerged. This reiterates the narrative information that the Turks have been taken completely by surprise. At the same time the epic sweep of this shot marks an exhilarating end to the first part of the narrative.

After this visual highpoint, things change. During the journey back to Cairo near to the start of the second part of the narrative, Lawrence, Daud, and Farraj get caught in a violent sandstorm which sometimes obscures the spectator's view of them altogether. This gives the first indication of a general shift in tone in the second part of the narrative. In the first part, sand is similarly blowing through the air when Lawrence, watched by Daud and Farraj, spends a night pondering how the Arabs might win a victory against the Turks. The wind abruptly stops blowing the sand behind him just before he exclaims, at the end of this sequence, 'Aqaba. Aqaba from the land.' Here the desert seems to submit to his will. The journey back to Cairo is the first time that it gets the better of him, with Daud dying in quicksand. When this journey ends and Lawrence and Farraj arrive at an abandoned outpost on the edge of the desert, the desolate tone is perpetuated through other means. Shot compositions in the outpost feature door frames, window frames, and netting in the foreground with Lawrence behind them. Lawrence at this point is silent, looking downcast. White make-up gives him a pallid, expressionless appearance. Shot compositions, elements of mise-en-scène, and performance combine to represent Lawrence as inaccessibly enigmatic, literally distanced from the spectator.

Cinematography and mise-en-scène in the second part of the narrative, as in the first, produce a variety of tones according to particular landscape and situations. Lawrence's first ambush of a Turkish train is brightly lit. At the end of this sequence, the first in which Jackson Bentley observes Lawrence in action, he walks triumphantly across the top of the train with his diaphanous robes illuminated by the sun above him (see Costume, and Genre: The male epic). However, the overall movement of the second part of the narrative is towards visual bleakness. The sequence at Deraa ends in near darkness, with Lawrence face down in the mud. The final leg of the Arab army's campaign, en route to Damascus, begins spectacularly with massed extras and colourful flags reminiscent of the earlier departure from Wadi Rhumm. Yet the atmosphere soon changes. A mixture of grey and dull blue rather than bright colour tones predominates after the massacre of the retreating Turkish platoon. Unlike the exhilarating capture of Aqaba, the Arab army's entry into Damascus is not shown at all.

realism, exoticism & subjectivity

In notes and letters written whilst scouting for locations and planning *Lawrence of Arabia*, David Lean recorded some of his intentions. These documents are quoted extensively in Kevin Brownlow's biography of Lean and in Adrian Turner's book on the making of the film. One thing Lean a realistic picture of the desert?

wrote about was his desire to represent the desert in a distinctive manner which would capture the magnificence and uniqueness of his chosen locations in Jordan. Lean felt that filming *Lawrence* in the locations which Lawrence actually traversed would help to give the film a realistic edge and set it apart from previous desert films (see Filmography). New technologies, such as the 65mm Panavision camera fitted with a 450mm lens used by Freddie Young for the Masturah well sequence, certainly produced some representations of the desert which were strikingly different from those in previous films.

Whether or not one agrees that *Lawrence* represents the desert in a more realistic manner than preceding films, it does contain distinctive stylistic features. During preproduction Lean wrote that, in the desert, 'everyone is somehow more out on their own there, and perhaps they just have to come face to face with themselves if they come under its spell. It's probably more dangerous for the town dweller, for as in Lawrence's case, the foundations are in dreams'. Here Lean indicates that, alongside his striving for realism, he wants his film to acknowledge that subjectivity and 'dreams' were an important part of Lawrence's desert experience. What he wants spectators to engage with is not just the desert itself. He also wants to bring into focus the relationship between Lawrence's subjectivity and the desert, or even the way the desert becomes a projection of Lawrence's subjectivity.

The style of the first two desert sequences in the narrative illustrates this intertwining of realism and subjectivity. Just prior to the first sequence, involving Lawrence's and Tafas's journey, Dryden delivers his 'you have a funny sense of fun' line of dialogue over a close-up of Lawrence blowing out a lighted match. This is the first close-up in a film where close-ups carry significant weight in relation to character subjectivity (see Close-ups). As the match goes out there is the famous cut to an extreme long shot of the sun slowly rising over a desert horizon (see Editing: Transitions between sequences). This is the first, astoundingly beautiful desert image in the film.

Dryden's dialogue about Lawrence's complex character traits and the close-up bringing us literally closer to the enigmatic Lawrence establish a context for the subsequent shot of the sun rising over the desert. The preceding dialogue and image imply that the desert in this film should be seen not only in realist terms but also as somehow an expression of Lawrence's desire. The sun rises as if in response to his action of blowing out the match, although the desert will later become a place where he will experience pain extending far beyond that caused by snuffing out a lighted match by hand. At this early point in the narrative Lawrence seems to have control over his destiny and power over the desert. The first desert sequence of Lawrence's and Tafas's journey represents the desert as a place of exoticism, beauty, and 'fun'. It is, initially, everything Lawrence had wished for.

The tone shifts in the second desert sequence at the Masturah well. It is less exotic than the first. Lawrence and Tafas peer into the far distance of the flat, bleak landscape around the well as an unidentifiable blur gradually transforms itself into Sherif Ali riding into the foreground from the horizon. Some of the extreme long shots here last for over twenty seconds, building up anticipation as the two men try to discern who or what is coming towards them. On the most obvious level this sequence advances the narrative by dramatically introducing the most significant Arab character within the film. It also makes dynamic use of the widescreen format in an attempt to represent realistically what a mirage might look like. At some points the sky melts into the sand and Sherif Ali seems to be riding across a shimmering sea. Yet as Steven Caton has argued in his analysis of this encounter, many elements in this sequence point towards the possibility that Ali is Lawrence's double.

The first shot in this sequence is taken from an unusual angle deep within the well. If the preceding sequence has linked the desert to Lawrence's subjectivity, then this shot from deep inside the landscape suggests that what is about to occur also relates to something deep inside him. Unlike the preceding, more lighthearted sequence, there is no nondiegetic music accompanying the Masturah well encounter. The only sound as Ali draws nearer is an eerie, barely audible swishing. This could be his camel's hooves across the sand, but it nevertheless produces an uncanny effect. Lawrence asks Tafas 'Who is he?'; a question asked of Lawrence himself several times in the narrative.

After Ali has shot Tafas and arrived in the foreground, shot compositions repeatedly frame Lawrence and Ali, two characters of similar age, height and build, facing each other in profile. Similar compositions recur throughout the film. Visually, the mysterious stranger who has just emerged from the desert to commit an act of violence mirrors Lawrence himself. On one level Ali is Lawrence's double, acting out his hidden impulses. The desert offers Lawrence a reflection of that part of himself which is drawn towards inflicting and enduring pain. Even in this first encounter between major European and Arab characters, the film can be interpreted as implying that violence is not simply innate to Arabs and to the desert (see Non-linear structures: Limitations of structuralism). The film enables it to be seen in a different way as a quality which Europeans deny in themselves and project onto other, supposedly less civilised cultures (see Ideology: Ambivalence).

editing

EDITING WITHIN SEQUENCES

Lawrence of Arabia conforms to the conventions of continuity editing The sequence representing the meeting of the Arab national council in the vast chamber in Damascus, for example, illustrates the sophisticated way in which editor Anne Coates and director Lean worked within these conventions. The sequence opens with an establishing shot which defines the space the action will unfold within. This is a long shot involving a tilt down and forward camera movement into the chamber where Lawrence, Ali, and Auda Abu Tayi sit at a table in the foreground with Arabs massed in the background.

The line formed by the characters in the foreground creates an 'axis of action'. Subsequent shots do not cross the line formed by the characters. Shots of Ali and Auda Abu Tayi shouting at each other are taken from the same side of the table as the establishing shot. This is crucial to continuity editing which assumes that crossing the line established by an axis of action will disorientate the spectator.

In general, continuity editing also aims to make the transitions between shots relatively smooth and imperceptible. Eyeline matches help to

editing style

achieve this. Auda Abu Tayi is looking and shouting towards screen left in the sequence's second shot, whereas Ali is looking and shouting towards screen right in the third. The direction of Auda Abu Tayi's look prepares the spectator for the transition to the shot of Ali, and the direction of Ali's look immediately links him to Auda Abu Tayi. Both also use their hands to gesture towards each other, and the cuts between shots occur at the precise moment when these gestures end.

Matches on action are also used to construct an impression of spatial and temporal continuity between shots. In other words, an action begun in one shot is sometimes matched in the next shot in order to reinforce the spectator's impression of coherent space and continuous time. In the sequence's fourth shot Auda Abu Tayi climbs onto the table, walks towards Ali, and crouches down to argue with him. Auda Abu Tayi's movement is continued in a fifth, closer shot. He then turns, walks out of the right hand side of the frame and into the left hand side of the frame in the sixth shot.

Although some of the shots in this sequence highlight individual characters, no close-ups are used. *Lawrence*'s widescreen format enables characters to be prominent within the shot without sacrificing background detail. This helps to maintain spatial continuity and, in this particular sequence, suggests that the arguments between individual characters have larger historical ramifications for the Arabs as a whole. Massed Arab extras appear in every shot in this sequence, responding to the arguments of their various leaders. The meeting of the Arab national council in the vast chamber in Damascus is one of several sequences in the film which represent history being determined through decisive individuals who hold sway over anonymous crowds of people (see Hollywood narratives: Character and history).

Whilst respecting the conventions of continuity editing, this sequence is also edited according to more abstract principles. It has its own rhythm and is structured symmetrically. It begins with a long shot in which the camera tracks forward into the chamber. It ends with a long shot in which the camera tracks backwards out of the chamber as Lawrence leaves, besieged by frantic petitioners. By opening and closing the sequence with these shots the editing moves the spectator through space and infuses this sequence with a sense of pace, shape and structure.

Approximately half way through this sequence there is an extreme long shot taken from high up in the gallery. This establishes a new axis of action, and also serves other functions. For the first and only time the extras stop gesticulating and become still. Win Ryder's sound editing is also crucial in this sequence. This is the one shot in which Lawrence, by banging his revolver on the table, manages to quiet the cacophony caused by the massed Arabs. The sound of the revolver banging on the table carries over from the preceding closer shot where Lawrence begins this action. There is little reduction in volume despite the change of visual perspective. The match on action also helps to smooth over the shift to a new axis of action. In the extreme long shot Lawrence delivers an impassioned plea:

Lawrence

>   We here are neither Harith nor Howeitat, nor
>   any other tribe but Arabs of the Arab Council,
>   acting for Prince Feisal!

Unlike the sequence's opening and closing shots, there is no camera movement in the extreme long shot in which Lawrence begins the delivery of this line of dialogue. It represents a momentary attempt to impose calm and order which is overwhelmed by the shots full of frenetic sound and movement surrounding it in this sequence.

TRANSITIONS BETWEEN SEQUENCES

Transitions between sequences in *Lawrence* develop narrative momentum and often operate on other levels as well. A straightforward, effective transition occurs at the end of Bentley's interview with Feisal. In this interview Bentley explains that he is looking for a story which will present American newspaper readers with the 'more adventurous aspects' of war. At this point America had not yet entered the First World War. The sequence concludes with a close-up of Feisal declaring 'Aurens [the Arabs' name for Lawrence] is your man'.

memorable images

Bentley's interview with Feisal makes the transition to the next sequence through an abrupt cut to a medium shot, in a desert location, of Lawrence pressing a plunger to explode a bomb under a passing Turkish train. This is followed by a series of shots of the train derailing, Lawrence and the Arab army firing on the ambushed train, Turkish soldiers returning fire, and Bentley snapping photographs. In addition to rapidly moving the narrative along, the parallels between Bentley's and the soldiers' shooting make the point that his camera, used to deliberately romanticise Lawrence's exploits, is not neutral (see Self-conscious romanticisation). It too is part of the machinery of war.

Other transitions brought about by Coates's and Lean's skilful editing construct a range of subtle effects and meanings. The famous cut between Lawrence blowing out a match in Cairo and the sun slowly rising over a desert horizon is an audacious one. It serves multiple purposes. In the narrative it signals a shift of location, and subsequent shots of Lawrence and Tafas crossing the desert on camels indicate that some time has passed between the end of the sequence in Cairo and the beginning of this one. Visually, the two shots are very different. One is a close-up, the other an extreme long shot. The background is out of focus and colour is subdued in the close-up, whereas colour is almost blindingly brilliant in the desert shot. These visual differences establish an opposition between city and desert locations (see Non-linear structures: Space).

Even in this famous cut, memorable because of graphic differences between the shots, there are elements of continuity. The match's small flame bears a tiny resemblance to the overpowering sun. Sound editing also prevents the contrast from being too stark and unsettling. The sound of Lawrence blowing out the match bridges the cut. It sets up a subliminal connection between the intimacy of the film's first close-up of Lawrence's face and the extreme long shot of the vast open space of the desert. Lawrence's action in the first shot is obliquely linked to the sun's movement in the next (see Realism, exoticism, and subjectivity).

The auditory link between Lawrence and the desert is reiterated on the soundtrack a few seconds later. Maurice Jarre's romantic music, including the film's famous 'Lawrence of Arabia' theme, gradually increases in volume as the sun rises. This musical theme has previously been heard over the opening credits which introduced the enigmatic Lawrence. Given the absence of nondiegetic music between the credits and this point, the theme's reappearance suggests that this is where Lawrence's 'fun' and adventure really begin, and that this is where more insight into his character might be gained.

The editing transition between Lawrence's and Tafas's desert journey and their arrival at the Masturah well also achieves a careful balancing of contrasts and continuities. Rather than a cut, which involves an instantaneous change from one shot to another, a dissolve is used for this transition between sequences. Dissolves superimpose the end of one shot over the beginning of the next and are often used to signify the passing of time. This is the case here, although the dissolve lasts longer than is usual. As is also the case here, dissolves can sometimes create specific emotional effects and establish conceptual links between different shots and sequences.

The final helicopter long shot of Lawrence's and Tafas's journey dissolves into a stationary low angle long shot from deep inside the Masturah well. The dissolve smoothes a contrast between the extreme high and low angles of these two long shots. Within the dissolve the centres of interest in both superimposed shots overlap. This aids continuity but also produces an uncanny effect. The two camel riders in the first shot seem to fly across the circle of sky formed by the top of the well in the centre of the second shot.

Ominously, the edges of the shot from inside the well are pitch black, and Jarre's romantic music fades out of the soundtrack just before Lawrence and Tafas peer down into the well. The strange, phantasmagoric effect momentarily created through the superimposition of these two shots is striking and unusual, like the match/rising sun cut. It also anticipates the eeriness of Ali's arrival (see Realism, exoticism, and subjectivity). Each example hints at the possibility that the desert experience represented in this film is on one level a reflection of Lawrence's dreams, fears, and desires. The desert in *Lawrence of Arabia* can be seen as a partly imaginary space, with its 'foundation in [European] dreams', as Lean put it (see

Ideology: Orientalism). If this is so, the helicopter shot/well interior dissolve might literally imply that these dreams, fears, and desires will lead Lawrence to hit the heights of pleasure and plumb the depths of despair.

close-ups

For a film lasting well over three hours, there are relatively few close-ups in *Lawrence of Arabia*. Their rarity, and the fact that the widescreen format makes them even larger than usual, gives them more significance and impact when they do occur. One of the ways the film's opening sequence establishes Lawrence as an enigma is by obscuring his facial expression, so subsequent close-ups of Lawrence's face offer the possibility of gaining at least some insight into his character and motivations (see Narrative circularity).

Significantly, close-ups tend to reveal Lawrence as tortured or traumatised by his involvement in inflicting or enduring pain. At the end of the sequence when he reports to Allenby after the capture of Aqaba, Lawrence falteringly admits that he 'enjoyed' the deaths of Gasim and Daud. Allenby responds by dismissing this as 'rubbish', but the close-up of Lawrence's troubled expression as he delivers this confession underlines its significance for the spectator. Similarly, there are a number of close-ups of Lawrence's face registering both fear and guilty enjoyment during the terrible massacre of the Turkish platoon just prior to the Arab army's arrival in Damascus.

The most concentrated use of close-ups in *Lawrence* takes place in the sequence where Lawrence is temporarily detained in Deraa and subjected to sexual violence by the Turkish bey there. Lawrence and Ali go to Deraa to spy on the Turks and to demonstrate Lawrence's courage and invincibility to the flagging Arab army. However this does not explain why, when they arrive in Deraa, Lawrence seems intent on drawing attention to himself and being captured by the Turks. One motivation could be the narcissism and exhibitionism Lawrence has previously displayed (see Costume, and Genre: The male epic). Another could be that he is unconsciously seeking punishment for the deaths of Gasim, Daud, Farraj,

'A man cannot be <u>always</u> in uniform'

and the violence he has become embroiled in. Yet paradoxically, as the incidents with lighted matches at the beginning of the narrative have already hinted, he enjoys enduring pain. The Deraa sequence revolves around Lawrence's ambivalent attraction to and revulsion from sadomasochistic practices.

Lawrence is apprehended by some Turkish soldiers and put into a line-up inspected by the Turkish bey. The bey picks Lawrence out and begins interrogating him. As he begins to strip Lawrence there is a close-up of the bey's long shiny boots of leather, which are part of the conventional paraphernalia of sadomasochistic practices. The bey rips open Lawrence's shirt to reveal his bare chest, and insists:

```
Bey

        Yes, you are a deserter

(smiling archly)

        but from which army? Not that it matters at
        all.

(with strange feeling)

        A man cannot be always in uniform.

He removes his right glove and taking Lawrence's
pectoral muscle between thumb and finger begins to
kneed [sic] it.
```

The Turkish bey's dialogue downplays the military and political context of this encounter and focuses attention on its looming sexual violence as he caresses and pinches Lawrence's chest.

The Turkish bey's dialogue about stepping out of uniform and the predominance of close-ups also suggest that what we might be seeing in this sequence is Lawrence's character stripped bare, metaphorically as well as literally. Following this are the most extreme close-ups in the film, of Lawrence's frightened eyes and the bey's lascivious mouth. Lawrence lashes out and the bey orders him to be flogged. As the flogging progresses there are a series of close-ups of Lawrence's face, staring intently ahead and trembling slightly. An unspecified amount of time is elided through a

The Turkish bey

cut to Ali waiting anxiously outside. Lawrence is eventually thrown out to land face down in the mud. It is possible that during this time Lawrence has been raped. Lean has suggested that this is what he wanted audiences to infer.

Lawrence's expression when suffering the Deraa beating recalls the one he wears when confessing his enjoyment of Gasim's and Daud's deaths to Allenby. It also anticipates close-ups of his face during the massacre of the Turkish platoon. Lawrence seems compelled to revisit violent scenarios throughout the narrative. His ambivalent feelings are emphasised by close-ups which perhaps give some insight into the sadomasochistic impulses motivating this fascinatingly enigmatic character.

If this is accepted as a possibility then it has consequences for the spectator's understanding of the chains of cause and effect within the narrative. To a certain extent some of the violence represented within the narrative can be seen as resulting, inadvertently, from Lawrence's sadomasochistic impulses. These sometimes lead him into dangerous situations which he loses control of. This is not to say that he alone is responsible for all of the violence inflicted upon himself or upon others. However, it does provide a more complex level of explanation which goes beyond assumptions about the inherently barbarous and violent nature of Middle Eastern cultures (see Non-linear structures: Structuralism and binary oppositions, and Ideology: Ambivalence).

performance & dialogue

There are many accomplished performances in *Lawrence of Arabia*. In his analysis of the film Steven Caton argues that Peter O'Toole's performance is often overtly foregrounded. Bentley's persistent photographing and his newspaper reports about Lawrence's exploits, and his subject's willing collaboration with this, draw attention to all of Lawrence's actions within the second part of the narrative as potential 'performances' (see Self-conscious romanticisation).

Even in the first part of the narrative, Lawrence is represented as an inveterate performer. He performs to himself when alone. In an incident which is not in the script, Lawrence begins singing the popular song 'The Man who Broke the Bank at Monte Carlo' en route to Prince Feisal's camp. He delights in the echoes of his voice the desert sends back to him. Once again the desert reflects Lawrence's personality until Colonel Brighton, who has been watching and listening without Lawrence being aware of his presence, interrupts to introduce himself. There is a similar encounter later in the narrative when Lawrence, admiring himself in his new Arab robes, runs into a bemused Auda Abu Tayi for the first time (see Costume, and Genre: The male epic).

O'Toole's delivery of some of some key lines of dialogue in the film augments this stress on performance. One example is his denunciation of Ali at the Masturah well as 'Greedy, barbarous, and cruel' (see Hollywood narratives). The passion in O'Toole's voice here comes across as a deliberately crafted effect. Before the full seriousness of the encounter with the Turkish bey at Deraa becomes apparent, O'Toole's facial expression and vocal delivery register a certain amount of enjoyment in his performance within a performance when he pretends to be a Circassian (belonging to a light-skinned people from the Caucasus). There is an undercurrent of 'playing a role' which, in a number of ways, is associated with O'Toole's performance as Lawrence throughout the film. This maintains his enigmatic aura whilst also representing him as something of an exhibitionist. We can never be sure who Lawrence is or whether he is performing.

costume

The use of costume within *Lawrence of Arabia* reinforces the notion of Lawrence's enigmatic, constantly shifting identity, as well as highlighting his narcissism and exhibitionism. Small details of costume indicate this. In his analysis of the film Steven Caton draws attention to the significance of headgear. Lawrence takes off his cap immediately before Ali's arrival at the Masturah well, thereby removing one of the conventional signs of a British officer's identity. He puts on an Arab

costume

headdress for the first time before beginning the perilous journey across the Nefud desert. When Lawrence returns to Cairo after capturing Aqaba, he meets Allenby while dressed in Arab robes. This exchange takes place:

```
Allenby
     What d'you mean by coming in here dressed like
     that? Amateur dramatics?
Lawrence has thrown himself back in his chair, very
upright under this onslaught of calculated
vulgarity, has retreated back into the fastness of
his glacial nature. His eyes flash contemptuously.
Lawrence
     Oh yes sir. Entirely.
Allenby (holds out his hand)
     Let me see that - hat - or whatever it is.
He takes the kafia and argyl, examining them with
apparent interest.
     Fascinating gear they wear. How d'you think
     I'd look in this, Harry?
Brighton (stiffly)
     Damn ridiculous, sir.
Allenby (looking at Lawrence and handing it back
quietly)
     Here, you keep it.
```

Allenby's momentary interest in Lawrence's headgear provides another example of how, in the sequence when Lawrence returns to Cairo to report the capture of Aqaba, the possibility of reconciling binary oppositions is raised (see Non-linear structures: Structuralism and binary oppositions). Allenby plays with the idea of combining Eastern and Western dress codes. Allenby's guarded fascination with Lawrence's appearance also reiterates Lawrence's appeal as both legend and spectacle (see Genre: The male epic).

The importance of headgear as a marker of identity carries through to the end of the narrative. After the failure of the Arab national council meeting

costume style

costume   style

Lawrence revels in the Arabs' adulation

Lawrence on top of
the derailed train

in Damascus, Lawrence goes to inspect the appalling conditions at the Turkish military hospital. His face is covered by his Arab headdress. When a British medical officer observes the scene, he mistakes Lawrence for a 'Filthy little wog' and slaps him across the face. Ironically, this is the first time within the narrative that Lawrence has been unequivocally mistaken for an Arab. In the eyes of the medical officer Lawrence has finally become the orientalist stereotype of the dirty, barbarous, cruel Arab who cares little about human life (see Ideology: Orientalism).

Changes of costume support narrative development in *Lawrence*. Thus after the incident at Deraa, Lawrence returns to British military headquarters in Jerusalem to ask Allenby to relieve him of his duties in the desert. During this sequence Lawrence wears an ill-fitting British uniform and makes a conspicuous attempt to integrate with the other officers. Yet, as Adrian Turner has noted, Lawrence's uniform is khaki, a colour reminiscent of the desert, whereas the other officers wear a very English green.

Costume changes, particularly those involving Arab dress, are also part of *Lawrence*'s presentation of spectacle. After rescuing Gasim Lawrence begins to unbutton his uniform and then falls to the ground exhausted. Later that evening, as Lawrence sleeps, Ali burns his old clothes. The next day Ali gives him distinctive white Arab robes. These signify his acceptance by the Arabs but, as with the uniforms in the Jerusalem sequence, the colour still marks him out as different from the people around him.

In the second part of the narrative there is a memorable moment when Lawrence turns himself into pure spectacle. Encouraged by Bentley, he gracefully walks across the carriage of the derailed Turkish train. Massed Arabs cheer and applaud him as he basks in their adulation. There is a shot of the shadow he casts on the ground and a shot of his body permeated by the sun's rays. Production designer John Box and costume designer Phyllis Dalton varied the texture of O'Toole's costumes in different shots and sequences in order to help achieve effects like this. Lawrence striding across the train becomes a legendary figure. The connection in these shots between Lawrence and the sun echoes the much earlier match/rising sun cut. The stark contrast between the triumphant, resplendently clothed Lawrence here and his naked, beaten body at Deraa makes the latter sequence all the more striking (see Genre: The male epic).

contexts

ideology

ORIENTALISM

The best-known critical analysis of representations of the Middle East is Edward Said's 1978 book *Orientalism*. Said analyses the ways in which 'the Orient' (the East) is something defined and constructed by Western representations and discourses. These representations and discourses are shaped by, and help to perpetuate, power relationships between dominant Western cultures and subordinate cultures defined as 'oriental'. Said's *Orientalism* focuses primarily on European literary and scholarly writings about 'the Orient', but some of the general points he makes are relevant to *Lawrence of Arabia*. Said argues that Western representations of 'the Orient' tend to define it in terms of absolute difference from its opposite, the Occident (the West). The West is taken as the norm, and the Orient's difference is often marked in negative terms.

If Said's analysis is applied to *Lawrence of Arabia*, then Lawrence's description of the Arabs as 'a silly people, greedy, barbarous, and cruel' can be seen as a statement which is neither innocent nor simply descriptive. It derives from a long tradition of orientalist thinking which assumes that such qualities are a defining feature of Arab culture. Orientalist thinking assumes fundamental distinctions between negative qualities inherent in oriental cultures and positive qualities embodied in occidental, Western cultures such as Britain, France and America. To describe Arabs as 'greedy, barbarous, and cruel' implies that the West is generous, civilised and kind. In *Orientalism* Said challenges this way of thinking. He argues that, during the nineteenth and early twentieth centuries, such distinctions provided justification for British and French imperial rule over large parts of the Middle East.

Another point Said makes is about how Western representations and definitions of 'the Orient' deal with history. 'The Orient' is usually seen as without history, or as being in a state of historical decline. The West, on the other hand, makes history. The West is modern and dynamic whereas 'the Orient' is static, timeless, or mired in tradition. The West is the place where history progresses. This view of history makes Western imperialism, in the Middle East and elsewhere, seem necessary, rational, and even beneficial to the people it is imposed upon. According to this logic the Orient must accept Western rule and guidance if it is to develop and progress.

There are a number of ways in which, particularly through its use of spectacle, the desert and the Arabs are marked as absolutely different from the West in *Lawrence*. In *Orientalism*, Edward Said argues that for many orientalist writers the desert is a privileged location because it can be represented as having no history. For these writers it is also the place where essential differences between Arab and Western culture can be most clearly observed. Both of these ideas are implied by the first image of Arabia in *Lawrence*; the sun slowly rising over a desert horizon. This image defines Arabia as a place governed by nature, in all its beauty and harshness, rather than by history. The sandstorms and the quicksand which kills Daud reiterate this initial impression.

There is much visual emphasis in *Lawrence* on the desert, and on colourful Bedouin costumes, but relatively little attention is given to Bedouin history, economy, or culture. Adrian Turner points out that, historically, Feisal's encampment was a fixed site with solid structures and a settled culture. However, the encampment is represented in *Lawrence* as a transient group of wild, colourful Bedouin horse and camel riders living in tents. Turner suggests the film makers calculated that audiences would find spectacular sequences highlighting Arabia's exotic difference more appealing than strict historical accuracy (see Ideology: The romance of the desert, and Cultural contexts: Audience).

The orientalist emphasis on spectacular representations of the desert and the Bedouin in *Lawrence* is ideologically significant. It marginalises other historically significant aspects of Arab culture from the period the film is set in. For example Arab city dwellers are only ever represented as inert background detail in *Lawrence*. They are never represented as important characters in their own right or as a social group with a significant role to play within the historical process. They appear briefly as extras in sequences set in Cairo and Damascus, wearing Western-style suits or less colourful clothes than the Bedouin. Arab city dwellers do not provide good material for spectacular desert exoticism displaying the essential difference of Arab culture. To give Arab urban culture prominence within the film would undermine the binary oppositions between Europeans and Arabs, city and desert, civilisation and barbarism which, to a certain extent, form part of its basic structure (see Non-linear structures: Structuralism and binary oppositions).

Auda Abu Tayi epitomises some quintessentially orientalist ideas about Arabs and Arab culture. He is the character who most obviously embodies orientalist notions about fundamental differences between Arab and Western culture. Although represented in many respects as a sympathetic character, Auda displays stereotypically 'oriental' traits. He reacts emotionally rather than intellectually. He is volatile and hot-tempered. He demonstrates ferocious swordsmanship when he kills a wounded Turkish soldier who tries to shoot Lawrence after his train is derailed. Unlike Lawrence, Auda is never troubled by the violence surrounding him. He accepts it as part of the natural condition of Arab life. Auda's unshakeable belief that Bentley's camera will steal his virtue if it takes his photograph establishes him as a superstitious primitive far removed from the modern world. Even Auda's physical difference from the European characters is emphasised by the prosthetic nose the actor Anthony Quinn wore for the role.

THE ROMANCE OF THE DESERT

Lawrence of Arabia can be related to a particular strand of orientalism which emphasises the romantic allure of the desert. This strand of orientalism is discussed in Chapter Five of Deborah Root's *Cannibal Culture*. Root argues that for some European and American writers, artists, and film makers, the desert's presumed closeness to nature, and the supposedly traditional, primitive lifestyle of the people living there, are attractive. The desert seems to offer an alternative to European and American norms, conventions and restrictions (see Ideology: Marginality and romantic orientalism, and Genre: The male epic). Lawrence is established at the beginning of the film's narrative as a character drawn towards the desert because he is a misfit within a British context. He perceives the desert as a place where he can experience an alternative, utopian world of beauty, exoticism, and 'fun'.

This way of seeing the desert is still orientalist. It maintains the belief in a fundamental difference between 'the Orient' and the West, but it values certain aspects of 'the Orient''s difference positively. On the most basic level, the spectacle of exotic difference can be valued for the sheer visual pleasure it offers. Film critic Dilys Powell conveys this when, reviewing *Lawrence*, she praises the cinematography's 'communication of ecstasy' through its representations of 'blood-orange sand', 'dust storms like the smoke-trails of a djinn', and 'the colours of heat'. Powell, in line with conventional orientalist thinking, associates the desert with nature rather than history, and with 'blood' and 'djinns'. The desert remains linked to negative qualities such as violence and primitive superstition. Yet Powell is also clearly captivated by the way the film makers have made it beautiful to behold.

MARGINALITY AND ROMANTIC ORIENTALISM

An issue to consider is the extent to which *Lawrence* encourages its spectator to think about Lawrence's subjectivity as one partly formed by orientalist assumptions. Does the film simply perpetuate, and attempt to immerse its spectator in, that strand of orientalism which subscribes to romantic visions of the desert? Alternatively, are these representations given a self-conscious, possibly critical edge? Is the film's spectator encouraged to reflect upon the reasons why Lawrence is drawn to the desert, and why he might seek to project his own orientalist preconceptions and expectations onto it? How thoroughly and systematically does the film question the orientalist representations of the desert which Lean described as having their 'foundation in [European] dreams' (see Realism, exoticism, and subjectivity, and Editing)?

Deborah Root points out that romantic desert orientalism holds particular appeal for white Westerners who, for a variety of reasons, are dissatisfied with or marginalised by Western culture. *Lawrence of Arabia* implies that one of the reasons for Lawrence's attraction to the desert and alienation

Lawrence's background disclosed

from British culture is his socially marginal status. The most explicit reference to this takes place after Lawrence has rescued Gasim in the Nefud desert and is beginning to be proclaimed a hero by the Arabs. They start to call Lawrence 'El Aurens'. As he rests, Ali strikes up a conversation with him about his new Arab name and his family background:

Ali (quietly)

    El Aurens ... Truly, for some men nothing is written unless they write it.

(it is capitulation)
Lawrence (moved, he laughs quietly, goes on eating. Then)

    Not 'El Aurens', Just Lawrence.

Ali

    El Aurens is better.

Lawrence

    True.

Ali

    Your father too? Just Mr. Lawrence?

Lawrence

(considers this. Pushes away the food. Turns on his back and closes his eyes as though asleep, and says with an effort)

    My father is Sir Thomas Chapman.

Ali (pleased)

    Is that a Lord?

Lawrence

    A kind of Lord.

Ali

    Then when he dies you too will be a Lord.

Lawrence

    No.

```
Ali (sympathetic)
     Ah. You have an elder brother.
(a common complaint among aristocrats like himself)
Lawrence
     No.
Ali
     But then ...
(another point strikes him)
     I do not understand this - Your father's name
     is Chapman -
Lawrence
     Ali. My father isn't really my father. He
     didn't marry my mother.
(the words 'father' and 'mother' come out on a
barely perceptible effort of breath)
Ali (gravely)
     I see.
(he is disturbed. He must think this out. Silence.)
Lawrence
     I'm sorry.
(and this is not bitter but a humble though
dignified apology for a fault.)
Ali
(after further thought; quietly)
     It seems to me that you are free to choose
     your own name then.
Lawrence
(he keeps his eyes tightly shut)
     Yes, I suppose I am.
Ali
(with a quick smile - and this is an act of real
moral generosity)
     'El Aurens' is best.
```

Lawrence

(after a pause in which he controls the surge of
gratitude – dangerously similar to love – which
rises in him)

    All right, I'll settle for 'El Aurens'.

This conversation is represented in medium close-ups of the two men, edited into a shot/reverse shot structure (see Close-ups). This one and only discussion of Lawrence's family background occurs at a crucial transitional point in narrative. The transformation of Lawrence's identity through his new costume and his new name, and his desire to integrate into Arab culture, are linked to a revelation of his marginal status within British culture. At the end of this sequence Ali burns Lawrence's old clothes, and there is a dissolve to the beginning of the next sequence where he dresses Lawrence in Arab robes for the first time.

This conversation provides some explanation for Lawrence's attraction to the desert as a place which might provide a viable alternative for him. Retrospectively, it clarifies why the only Western characters Lawrence seems comfortable with are the working-class sergeant and corporal in the map-making room in Cairo at the beginning of the narrative. Like him they have little social status. It also helps to explain why Lawrence quickly bonds with Daud and Farraj. As orphans and outcasts they are marginal characters within the Bedouin community. In his conversation with Lawrence, Ali concludes that Lawrence's family background leaves him free to make his own name. The spectator can reasonably infer that Lawrence's attraction to the desert and his desire to make history there emerge partly from a wish to escape the British social norms which marginalise him.

AMBIVALENCE

Earlier in the narrative, just before he hits on the idea of attacking Aqaba by land, Lawrence has a conversation with Feisal in his tent. Several points Feisal makes directly challenge orientalist assumptions:

Feisal

> You are an Englishman. Are you not loyal to
> England?

Lawrence

(hesitates, smiles a smile of intellectual, not
emotive humour)

> To England and to other things.

But Feisal will not play the intellectual game,
though amply intellectual — for him the question is
practical, and his expression is serious as he draws
up to Lawrence and says thoughtfully:

Feisal

> To England and Arabia both? And is that
> possible ...?

(he approaches Lawrence closely and considers him.
He nods)

> I think you are another of these desert-loving
> Englishmen —

(he walks away)

> Doughty, Stanhope, Gordon of Khartoum.

(he turns)

> No Arab loves the desert. We love water and
> green trees.

> There is nothing in the desert. And no man
> needs nothing.

(His tone changes from the philosophic to the
emotional)

> ... or is it that you think we are something
> you can play with because we are a little
> people, a silly people; greedy, barbarous and
> cruel?

'Time to be great again'

(Lawrence looks surprised)

> But you know, Lieutenant, in the Arab city of
> Cordova were two miles of public lighting in
> the streets – when London was a village!

Lawrence

> Yes, you were great.

Feisal (dryly)

> Nine centuries ago.

Lawrence (mildly)

> Time to be great again my Lord.

Feisal (stiffly)

> Which is why my father made this war upon the
> Turks –
>
> my father, Mr Lawrence, not the English!

(he is suddenly overcome by melancholy)

> But my father is old and I – I long for the
> vanished gardens of Cordova

(sighs)

> However, before the gardens must come the
> fighting.

He indicates graciously the tent flap. They move
over to it, and Feisal courteously holds it apart.

Feisal (with formal politeness, smiling)

> To be great again, it seems we need the
> English or ...

(he shrugs)

Lawrence (gently)

> Or ...?

Feisal (looking over the silent encampment)

> What no man can provide, Lieutenant. We need a
> miracle.

Feisal challenges orientalist assumptions

Feisal is represented as a shrewd, intelligent man, aware of the romantic orientalist tradition of 'desert-loving Englishmen'. Lawrence does not reject Feisal's suggestion that he is part of this tradition. By contrasting British 'desert-lovers' with another, far less romantic Arab perception of the desert, Feisal highlights how Lawrence belongs to a particular tradition of seeing the desert 'through Western eyes'. Feisal also points out another limitation in Lawrence's orientalist perception of Arabs. He ridicules the generalisation Lawrence made at the Masturah well about their 'greedy, barbarous and cruel' nature. This comment is later turned back on Lawrence for a second time. Ali reminds him of it after the final massacre of the Turkish platoon (see Character transformations). Feisal's and Ali's use of this phrase critically underlines how, through orientalist thinking, Westerners generalise about Arab culture and project negative qualities onto it which they prefer to deny within their own cultures.

Feisal also raises the issue of historical agency in his conversation with Lawrence. A standard orientalist assumption is that 'the Orient' must be led by the West because it cannot make its own history. Feisal is aware of this assumption, and challenges it by emphasising that it was his father, not the English, who 'made this war upon the Turks'. Feisal argues that Arabs can make their own history. At the same time, his reference to the 'vanished gardens of Cordova' from 'nine centuries ago' suggests that he subscribes to the orientalist idea of 'the Orient' being in a state of long-term historical decline. A similar ambivalence emerges towards the end of the conversation. Despite having forcefully argued that Arabs are active historical agents, rather than inert objects acted upon by the West, Feisal concedes that 'we need the English'. Lawrence then wanders out into the desert to devise his plan for capturing Aqaba. He assumes, in typically orientalist fashion, that he can provide the 'miracle' Feisal refers to.

Feisal is represented throughout *Lawrence*'s narrative as a canny politician. He is well aware that the British are in a dominant position, but skilfully tries to extract maximum advantage from the situations he finds himself in. Feisal's discussions with Lawrence, Bentley, Allenby and Dryden demonstrate his sophisticated understanding of Western culture. All three discussions touch upon the issue of representation. Feisal understands the

Lawrence's image exploited

power and influence that particular representations can have within Western culture.

In his final negotiations with Allenby and Dryden, after Lawrence has left the scene, Feisal reminds them that 'it is widely known the Arab Council took power [in Damascus] in my name'. Thanks to Bentley's reporting, which Feisal encouraged, 'the world is delighted with the picture of Damascus liberated by the Arab army' (see Self-conscious romanticisation). Feisal draws attention to a romanticised photograph of Lawrence on the front page of an American newspaper. When Allenby reminds him that Lawrence is a British officer, Feisal counters by saying 'Aurens is a sword with two edges'.

This is a subtle exchange within a negotiation to decide the allocation of British, French and Arab power and territory within the newly liberated Middle East. What Feisal suggests, through his reference to Lawrence as 'a sword with two edges', is that orientalist representations are never entirely one-sided. Allenby knows it will serve British interests if Lawrence's photograph in the newspaper is interpreted as confirmation of an orientalist narrative in which a heroic British officer has conquered the desert and led the Arabs to a great victory they could not have achieved on their own. Feisal, who significantly refers to Lawrence by his Arab name 'Aurens', emphasises that Lawrence has identified completely with the Arab cause. Lawrence is 'a sword with two edges' because, if encouraged to do so by Feisal, he could become an influential advocate for Arab demands for power and territory.

Steven Caton, in his analysis of the conversation between Lawrence and Feisal in Feisal's tent, argues that it is staged, shot and edited to suggest that Feisal manipulates Lawrence from the outset. Feisal immediately realises that Lawrence is a 'desert-loving Englishman', captivated by romantic orientalist representations of the desert. Feisal consciously plays upon Lawrence's orientalist preconceptions about 'the Orient'. He nurtures the idea, derived from orientalist thinking, that Lawrence might be able to provide the 'miracle' which would make the Arabs great again. Feisal's campaign against the Turks has reached an impasse at this point in the narrative. He has nothing to lose by trying to mobilise whatever help he can get in any way he can.

filmography

There are many aspects of *Lawrence* which demonstrate a critical self-consciousness in relation to orientalist representations. Attentive spectators can reflect upon subtleties such as Feisal's understanding of these representations and his attempts to turn them, as far as possible, to his own advantage. It is even possible to argue that Auda Abu Tayi's apparently primitive and superstitious fear that Bentley's camera will steal his virtue is vindicated by the film. Lawrence opens himself up to the media, and his image becomes something which Feisal, Allenby, Dryden and others struggle to control and define. Lawrence himself is left without a clear identity at the end of the film. However, it is important to reiterate that, although these are all plausible interpretations, they are also subtle, implicit ones. They are the kind of interpretations the spectator may arrive at after careful reflection or after repeat viewings of the film.

It can be argued that *Lawrence of Arabia* implies that Lawrence's marginality within British culture partly explains the appeal of romantic orientalism for him. It can also be argued that the film is self-conscious and ambivalent about orientalist representations and its own relationship to this way of understanding the Middle East. Nevertheless *Lawrence* does not and, given the generic expectations attached to such an expensive and ambitious film project, cannot develop a coherent alternative to orientalism. *Lawrence's* commercial viability as an epic film depends, to a large extent, upon the orientalist spectacles of exotic difference it stages for its spectator's visual pleasure (see Filmography, and Industrial).

filmography

EPICS AND 'ANTI-EPICS'

A group of films *Lawrence of Arabia* can be related to is the cycle of epics produced by Hollywood during the 1950s and early 1960s. These include religious epics such as *The Ten Commandments* (Cecil B. de Mille, 1956), Roman epics such as *Spartacus* (Stanley Kubrick, 1960), medieval epics such as *El Cid* (Anthony Mann, 1961), and contemporary historical epics such as *Exodus* (Otto Preminger, 1960).

For a brief period Hollywood invested heavily in epic production. One of the reasons for this was competition from television. The epic was a genre in which new technologies such as Cinemascope could display armies of extras, lavish costumes, and extravagant sets. These resources were mobilised to produce spectacles far more overwhelming than anything possible on television. Another reason for the emphasis on Hollywood epics set or filmed in foreign locations was that labour costs were often cheaper abroad during this period. International casts and grand narratives drawn from the full range of world history were reckoned to be of more interest to foreign audiences. Appealing to foreign as well as American audiences became more of a priority as Hollywood lost some of its domestic audience to television and other new leisure pursuits in the 1950s and early 1960s.

Hollywood epics were staggeringly ambitious projects. Publicity and advertising for them repeatedly drew attention to the extraordinary amount of human labour and material resources invested in and displayed within these films. Michael Wood, in Chapter Eight of his book *America in the Movies*, argues that at the most fundamental level the Hollywood epic is about American economic power, technological sophistication, conspicuous consumption and global superiority. Epic films involve the conspicuous display and often, in battle and disaster sequences, conspicuous destruction of spectacular resources. They operate on a scale on which only the American film industry could consistently afford to operate.

Hollywood used this power to represent various moments from world history, and films such as *The Ten Commandments*, *Exodus*, and *Lawrence* narrated very specific versions of ancient and modern Middle Eastern history. The one Middle Eastern film industry with the resources to produce an epic which narrates history from an Arab perspective was the Egyptian cinema. *Saladin* (Youssef Chahine, 1963) represents the defeat of medieval crusaders by a legendary Egyptian hero. It contrasts pointedly with the Christian victories against the Moors in *El Cid*, released two years earlier.

Like any film genre, Hollywood epics are not homogeneous, and distinctions need to be made between individual films. In 'Surge and Splendor', her critical essay on the Hollywood epic, Vivian Sobchack argues that European film makers often bring a different perspective to this genre. Her examples are *Walker* (Alex Cox, 1987) and *The Last Emperor* (Bernardo Bertolucci, 1987), and *Lawrence* could also be included here. Although

Lawrence as an 'anti-epic'

partly financed by Columbia, a Hollywood studio, Lean, the scriptwriter Robert Bolt, the majority of the production team, and many of the actors were British. Steven Caton has argued that *Lawrence*, particularly its second half, could even be described as an 'anti-epic'. It is desolate as well as spectacular and ends anti-climactically (see Narrative circularity, and Cinematography and mise-en-scène). The significant British contribution to the film could be one of the reasons for this.

The context Caton cites as one reason for *Lawrence's* anti-epic aspects is that the film went into production towards the end of the 1950s and early 1960s Hollywood epic cycle. *The Fall of the Roman Empire* (Anthony Mann, 1964) is another late film in this cycle which could also be described as containing 'anti-epic' elements. Publicity and advertising for epics produced during this period routinely claimed that each film was unique and exceptional, but generic cycles can eventually be perceived by audiences as conventional, predictable, and boring. Film makers working on *Lawrence* would have been aware that this epic cycle would eventually come to an end and that variations of the genre were necessary to retain audience interest. Shortly after *Lawrence* was released the epic *Cleopatra* (Joseph Mankiewicz, 1963) was a financial disaster. This encouraged Hollywood to move away from its previous emphasis on epic productions.

Aspects of *Lawrence* can be described as 'anti-epic', but the extent to which it can be enjoyed in terms of more conventional epic values should not be underestimated. The film was expensive to make, and the film makers aimed to attract a large audience who would expect a Hollywood epic set in the Middle East to include spectacular displays of orientalist difference (see Ideology: Orientalism, Production history, and Cultural contexts: Audience).

Posters for the film attempt to entice a potential audience into the cinema to enjoy spectacular pleasures. The one reproduced overleaf makes clear what *Lawrence* has to offer. On the left side of the poster are images of the film's impressive array of male stars. Their names, and 'TECHNICOLOR' and 'SUPER PANAVISION 70', two of the technological innovations used to produce the film's spectacular representations, are highlighted in bold lettering at the bottom. The right side of the poster depicts a line of Arab camel and horse riders. This is a clear promise of spectacular orientalist

Columbia Pictures Presents THE SAM SPIEGEL-DAVID LEAN Production of

LAWRENCE OF ARABIA

STANDS ALONE!

UNANIMOUSLY ACCLAIMED AS
"ONE OF THE ALLTIME GREAT FILMS!"
Winner of **7** Academy Awards
including
BEST PICTURE!

GUINNESS · ANTHONY QUINN · JACK HAWKINS · JOSE FERRER · ANTHONY QUAYLE · CLAUDE RAINS · ARTHUR KENNEDY with OMAR SHARIF as "Ali" and introducing PETER O'TOOLE as "LAWRENCE"

SCREENPLAY BY ROBERT BOLT · PRODUCED BY SAM SPIEGEL · DIRECTED BY DAVID LEAN · A HORIZON PICTURE IN TECHNICOLOR · PHOTOGRAPHED IN SUPER PANAVISION 70° C

Poster for *Lawrence of Arabia*

characteristics of the 'male epic'

difference and an invitation to marvel at the resources the film makers and the film industry supporting them have mobilised to make the film. Interestingly, however, the most prominent element of spectacle in this poster is an image of Lawrence himself, dressed in Arab robes.

genre

THE MALE EPIC

The epic film is often considered to be a predominantly 'male' genre. *Lawrence of Arabia* has no female characters. Women are rarely present even as extras. This makes the film fertile ground for an exploration of masculinity. *Lawrence* can be related to a group of Hollywood films from the early 1960s which Leon Hunt in his essay 'What are Big Boys Made of?' has described as 'male epics'. Hunt defines the Hollywood 'male epic' in terms of four characteristics:

■ Firstly, the films feature and are usually named after a heroic male protagonist. *Ben-Hur* (William Wyler, 1959), *El Cid* and *Spartacus* are examples of this.

■ Secondly, the hero becomes, or strives to become, more than an ordinary man. In *Lawrence* this ideal is the Lawrence/ 'Aurens' name and legend.

■ Thirdly, as the *Lawrence* poster suggests, the male epic involves displaying the male body.

■ Finally, the male epic represents what could be described as love stories between men. In *Lawrence* the Lawrence-Ali relationship fits into this category.

LOOKING AT LAWRENCE

One of the most important areas of debate within contemporary film theory derives from Laura Mulvey's essay 'Visual Pleasure and Narrative Cinema'. This is a famous analysis of 'the look' and 'the male gaze' in Hollywood cinema. Mulvey argues that, insofar as characters within Hollywood film narrative are concerned, it tends to be men who look whereas women are looked at. However *Lawrence of Arabia*, like other 'male epics', often overtly represents Lawrence as an object of the look. In

Mulvey's terms Lawrence is 'feminised' because he is marked as someone to be looked at by male characters and male audiences within the narrative, and by the film's spectator.

The first moment when Lawrence's 'to be looked at-ness' becomes explicit is when Ali dresses him in Arab robes after their conversation about Lawrence's family background (see Ideology: Marginality and romantic orientalism). The other Arabs who have crossed the Nefud with Lawrence begin to call him 'Aurens'. Lawrence canters off an a camel, dismounts, then runs with arms outstretched behind him as if about to fly. He regards his new identity admiringly, using the blade of his dagger as a mirror, but is startled by Auda Abu Tayi who has been silently watching him. This sequence constructs a pleasurable spectacle out of Lawrence's shifting identity. It also demonstrates, through Auda, that the process of being looked at is something Lawrence cannot entirely control.

Lawrence's narcissism is inseparable from exhibitionism in this film. His self-regard depends upon being looked at admiringly by others. One moment when the display of Lawrence's body for an audience within the film seems to raise him up to the status of a legendary, invincible hero is when he walks across the carriages of the ambushed Turkish train. At this point he appears supremely powerful, enamoured with himself, and in complete control of the process. Massed Arabs below chant 'Aurens', 'Aurens', whilst light from the sun above gives Lawrence a godlike glow (see Costume). He clearly derives narcissistic pleasure from this adulation.

Later in the narrative the consequences of being a figure who is looked at becomes more problematic, for example when Lawrence desperately tries to fight his way through an audience of frantic petitioners as he leaves the chamber where the Arab national council has convened. The most traumatic instance is when Lawrence is forcefully turned into a passive spectacle and his naked body is put on display for the Turkish officer and his men at Deraa (see Close-ups). Previously he has exercised some control over the situations in which his body has become an object of display. He is active and chooses to display himself in Arab robes. At Deraa his active role, his costume, and his ability to choose are brutally taken from him.

There are other moments when Lawrence is admired by characters and audiences within the film. When the men in the officers' bar in Cairo realise that he has taken Aqaba, they form an admiring audience, congratulating Lawrence as he and Farraj leave the bar. Even Allenby, a most unlikely admirer, is momentarily fascinated by Lawrence's Arab headgear during his subsequent debriefing (see Costume). What is significant about the admiring looks British male audiences and characters direct towards Lawrence is that they are relatively restrained compared to how non-European audiences and characters look at him within the film. It is the latter who most openly express wild excitement and sexual desire.

Lawrence contains a range of male characters and audiences looking at its hero in different ways. It could be argued that the film implies that there are 'legitimate' and 'illegitimate' ways of looking at Lawrence. The implications of this could be seen as orientalist (see Ideology: Orientalism). This argument is elaborated in the section of Ella Shohat's and Robert Stam's book *Unthinking Eurocentrism* entitled 'The Desert Odyssey'. Shohat and Stam argue that films set in 'the Orient' often play with conventional notions of gender roles and represent characters looking at each other in ways which would be 'illegitimate' in films set in the West.

Shohat and Stam argue that this serves two purposes. On the one hand, oriental settings provide a pretext for the spectator to enjoy sexual representations and looks which would be taboo in a Western context. On the other hand, it reinforces the message that these are not possible or permissible in the West, and that 'the Orient' is a negative, deviant space. Penelope Gilliat implies this when she writes in her review of *Lawrence* that 'one of the reasons for Lawrence's passion for Arab life might well have been that it allowed him to wear a skirt'. The assumption is that for a man to wear a skirt in a Western context would be unthinkable.

To a certain extent Shohat's and Stam's argument can be applied to *Lawrence*. British characters and audiences within the film, such as Allenby and the men in the officers' bar in Cairo, look at Lawrence with admiration but also with restraint. Arab and non-European audiences' and characters' looks at Lawrence, and the consequences of these looks, are often more 'excessive'. The most extreme example of this occurs at Deraa, where

Lawrence and Ali

Lawrence is subjected to the controlling, homosexual gaze of the Turkish bey. Although throughout *Lawrence* the film's hero is presented as a spectacle the sequence at Deraa epitomises, for the film's spectator, the 'wrong' way to look at Lawrence and the negative consequences of such an 'illegitimate' look.

A factor which complicates these issues, however, is the fourth point Leon Hunt makes about 'male epics'. *Lawrence*, like several other Hollywood 'male epics' from this period, contrasts an 'illegitimate' with a 'legitimate' relationship between men. The encounter between Lawrence and the Turkish bey is clearly the 'illegitimate' one, whereas the relationship between Lawrence and Ali is represented by the film as passionately 'legitimate'. If this contrast is focused on, then the encounter between Lawrence and the Turkish bey can be seen in a different light. Rather than demonstrating the film's orientalism and homophobia, the main reason why this encounter is represented as frightening and traumatic is because it involves a violent abuse of power.

The doubling of Lawrence and Ali, and the exchange of character traits which takes place between them as the narrative progresses, could be seen as undermining orientalism (see Character transformations, and Realism, exoticism and subjectivity). Their close relationship becomes more important than the fact that one is British and the other Arab. There are implicitly homosexual elements within their relationship, but it is represented as completely valid because of the love between them.

Ali's first act of tenderness towards Lawrence occurs after their conversation about Lawrence's family background. Ali tries to bolster Lawrence by suggesting that, since he doesn't carry his father's surname, 'you are free to choose your own name'. When Lawrence falls asleep, Ali throws his British officer's uniform onto a nearby fire. The next morning Ali helps Lawrence to put on white Arab robes which, as several critics have noted, resemble a bridal gown. There is delight on Ali's and the other Arabs' faces as Lawrence rides away. From this point onwards the film is punctuated with shots of Ali looking at Lawrence with desire, admiration, and concern. He sometimes seems on the verge of tears as he empathises with Lawrence's despair in the latter part of the narrative.

Ali's and Lawrence's last moment together in the film is especially poignant. It is late in the evening and Ali leaves Lawrence alone in the chamber where the failed Arab national council meeting took place. Ali strides into the background of the shot, turns, and bows farewell to Lawrence. As Ali exits Lawrence waves a halfhearted goodbye just a second too late for him to see it. When Ali has gone, the shot concludes with Lawrence turning back towards the camera with an absolutely devastated expression upon his face.

Scriptwriter Michael Wilson noted that Lean compared the Lawrence-Ali relationship to the 'deeply felt but unconsummated' one between the characters Alec and Laura in his earlier film *Brief Encounter* (1945). In that film some shots are composed in terms of painful distances between characters who never fully express or act upon their desire for each other. In both *Lawrence* and *Brief Encounter* mise-en-scène and the performance of the actors give many subtle indications of how strong this desire is. These indications can make the spectator wish that, against all the odds, the characters could stay together and develop their relationships further.

LIVING UP TO A NAME

Leon Hunt argues that the 'male epic' usually involves the central protagonist trying to live up to an impossible masculine ideal summed up by a name such as 'El Cid', 'Spartacus', or in this case Lawrence/ 'Aurens'. Becoming, or striving to become this ideal, often leads to the hero's death or destruction. Lawrence, deprived of the authority and status his aristocratic father's surname would have given him, tries to make a name for himself through his desert exploits (see Ideology: Marginality and romantic orientalism). Yet the burden of trying to live up to this heroic masculine ideal, of trying to be the great Lawrence/ 'Aurens', weighs heavily on Lawrence in the second part of the narrative. Others put pressure on him to live up to his name. Typically this is done out of self-interest, as when Allenby persuades Lawrence to return to the desert after his experience at Deraa. He shrewdly appeals to Lawrence's narcissism, describing him as an 'extraordinary' man. Similarly, Bentley plays upon Lawrence's exhibitionism by photographing him as a godlike figure.

Ali also puts pressure upon Lawrence to live up to his name. After Deraa, when Lawrence expresses his wish to give up and be an ordinary man again, Ali reminds him of his earlier claims that a man can be and do whatever he wants. Ali urges Lawrence to carry on when he falters. However, Ali is also the one character who perceives and shares some of the pain Lawrence experiences as a result of the burden these immense expectations impose on him. In this respect Ali, who shifts between these two ways of looking at Lawrence, illustrates two of the ways the film's spectator can look at him. Lawrence's attempt to live up to his name, to a heroic masculine ideal, can be admired. If this is the case, the ideal is validated. Alternatively, the attempt can be regarded as ultimately not worth the effort because of the evident pain it causes Lawrence.

After leaving Lawrence for the last time, Ali says to Auda Abu Tayi 'If I fear him [Lawrence] ... who love him ... How must he fear himself, who hates himself?' This is arguably a profound insight into Lawrence's state of mind by the one character in the film who really loves and understands him. In the preceding sequence Auda Abu Tayi has asked Lawrence whether he is traumatised and disillusioned because of the blood he has seen. Auda, the most stereotypically orientalist Arab in the film, blandly makes the orientalist statement that violence is innate to desert life: 'I tell you the desert has dried up more blood than you could think of' (see Ideology: Orientalism). Ali's final comment on Lawrence's character is more perceptive.

Ali suggests that Lawrence's trauma and self-hatred come from within, not from the desert. Ali knows, from their earlier conversation about his family background, that Lawrence's reasons for wanting to construct a new, ideal identity are rooted in his own personal and cultural background (see Ideology: Marginality and romantic orientalism). What Lawrence 'fears and hates' in himself is that his efforts to live up to the impossible masculine ideal of the orientalist hero have immersed him in more violence than he can cope with. When he first assumed this new identity and his new name 'Aurens', Lawrence enjoyed using the blade of his dagger as a mirror in which to admire himself. After the final attack on the Turkish platoon a disorientated, horrified Lawrence stares at his reflection in the same bloodstained dagger. Then Ali gently leads him away from the scene of the massacre which Lawrence, not the desert, is responsible for.

industrial

Lawrence of Arabia is a technically accomplished film. An understanding of the industrial conditions and cultural contexts within which the film took shape can help to explain why this is the case. *Lawrence* was an independent production. Sam Spiegel's Horizon Pictures was the production company, with the Hollywood studio Columbia acting as a financier and distributor.

Independent production companies such as Horizon flourished after the Second World War. Several factors encouraged this trend. These included changes in US tax laws which favoured producers, stars, directors, and writers investing earnings in their own independent production companies rather than remaining as salaried workers directly employed by major Hollywood studios. From the studios' perspective, the postwar decline in domestic US audiences led to a scaling down of the total number of films produced. This was accompanied by more emphasis on innovation and diversity, within certain limits, in order to attract audiences to the cinema (see Filmography). The policy, followed by Hollywood studios in the 1930s, of mass production of many films made less economic sense under these new market conditions. Major studios such as Columbia entered into short-term deals to distribute individual films from independent producers such as Horizon.

One consequence of the postwar shift towards independent production was that some actors, film makers, and film technicians became more mobile and able to work on a wider range of film projects than in the 1930s when employment on a longer-term basis by the major studios was the norm. For less well-known film workers this resulted in a loss of job security. Independent producers could now put together a package of film workers from anywhere in the industry, and indeed from all over the world. In the 1930s producers were generally restricted to employees of the particular studio they worked for. Sam Spiegel took full advantage of this new flexibility when putting together *Lawrence*'s production team.

a new epic for new audiences

Sam Spiegel and David Lean were in a particularly strong position after the success of Horizon's *The Bridge on the River Kwai* (1957), also distributed by Columbia. Spiegel and Lean were both awarded Oscars. *Kwai's* success made it possible for the producer-director team of Spiegel and Lean to continue making epic films. The next project they completed together was *Lawrence*. Bolstered by *Kwai's* success, and the financing this enabled him to obtain, Spiegel was able to assemble what film critic Alexander Walker described as an 'unbeatable team' of top industry professionals. In addition to several major stars, this team included Lean, cinematographer Freddie Young, upcoming new talent such as editor Anne Coates, and highly regarded specialists such as sound editor Win Ryder who had already worked with Lean on many of his previous films (see Background: Key players' biographies, and Production history).

With the postwar decline in domestic US audiences, box office takings from foreign audiences became more important to Hollywood producers (see Filmography). Steven Caton argues that one of the reasons why *Lawrence* is not a straightforwardly orientalist film is because of an increasing awareness of the sensibilities of non-American audiences. Added to this, Caton argues that American audiences were themselves becoming more sophisticated in their view of the rest of the world. This was partly due to American servicemen's involvement in the Second World War and the postwar expansion of business travel and tourism.

For the film makers involved in the project, there was clearly a balance to be struck in the production of *Lawrence*. One of the epic genre's most enduring points of appeal was spectacle. Spectacle in Hollywood epic films set in the Middle East traditionally involved representations highlighting the exotic, orientalist differences of Middle Eastern locations and characters (see Ideology: Orientalism, and Ideology: The romance of the desert). *Lawrence* is a film which responds to an industrial and cultural context requiring both sophisticated representations of the non-Western world and pleasurable spectacles of exotic orientalist difference (see Ideology: Ambivalence, and Filmography).

production history

Lawrence of Arabia was an ambitious project, several years in the making, which incorporated contributions from many talented people. Kevin Brownlow's, Steven Caton's, and Adrian Turner's books contain detailed accounts of the film's production. Autobiographies, biographies, and interviews with leading contributors also contain valuable information. Each and every contributor's input cannot be properly acknowledged here. The three aspects of the film's production history discussed below do not cover all departments of the film's production. Script, casting, reediting and restoration have been selected because they provide further insight into the complexities of the film discussed throughout this Note.

SCRIPT

In 1995 the Writers Guild of America ruled that credit for the *Lawrence of Arabia* screenplay should be shared by two writers, Michael Wilson and Robert Bolt. Previously screen credit had gone to Bolt alone. The Writers Guild ruling was the result of many years' lobbying by Wilson and his family. Both writers made significant contributions to the project, but film historians differ in their assessments of the quality and extent of each one's contribution. It has been common practice throughout Hollywood's history for more than one writer to work on a screenplay. The various writers contributing to this process do not always receive screen credit, and disputes sometimes arise.

Wilson's case was complicated because of his blacklisting by the HUAC (House Un-American Activities Committee) in the 1950s. Established during the height of the Cold War between the USA and the USSR, the HUAC called known or suspected Communist party sympathisers working within Hollywood to testify about their political activities and commitments. People called before the HUAC were also asked to 'name names'. They were asked not only about their own but also about their friends' and colleagues' political affiliations. Wilson refused to attend when he was called to the hearings. Hollywood studios adopted a policy of blocking employment or screen credit to people who did this. Wilson, like others who refused to testify, left America to go into exile in Europe.

changing perception of Lawrence

This dispute about Wilson's and Bolt's contributions to *Lawrence*'s screenplay has obscured what both writers have in common. Bolt, like Wilson, was on the left. He was a member of the Communist party for a short while in the 1940s and was briefly imprisoned for taking part in a CND (Campaign for Nuclear Disarmament) demonstration whilst working on the *Lawrence* screenplay. As left wing writers, Bolt and Wilson were both critical of British imperialism and cautiously supportive, at least in principle, of Arab nationalism. The 1956 Suez crisis strengthened these convictions. Egypt's President Nasser nationalised the Suez canal and led resistance to an ill-advised British, French and Israeli invasion of Egypt. Left wing intellectuals such as Wilson and Bolt tended to view the Suez crisis as the last gasp of an outdated, unjustifiable European imperialist attitude towards the Middle East. This coloured their view of Lawrence's activities during the First World War.

The changing literary representation of Lawrence also shaped Wilson's and Bolt's work. Both writers used *The Seven Pillars of Wisdom* (1935), Lawrence's own account of his exploits, as their main source text. Lawrence's fame was first established by the American publicist and journalist Lowell Thomas, who toured with a popular travelogue show about the desert campaigns in the years immediately after the end of the First World War. Thomas's book *With Lawrence in Arabia* (1924) became a bestseller. The Jackson Bentley character in the film is partly modelled upon him.

For Wilson and Bolt, working on a version of Lawrence's story in the late 1950s and early 1960s, Richard Aldington's: *Lawrence of Arabia: A Biographical Enquiry* (1955) was the most influential recent account of the film's enigmatic hero. Aldington's controversial book argued that Lawrence exaggerated or lied about many of the events he claimed to be involved in, and that he colluded in the construction of his own legend. Aspects of this argument influenced both Wilson's and Bolt's work on the *Lawrence* screenplay.

CASTING

Lawrence of Arabia had to feature an international cast of stars in order to appeal to as wide a range of audiences as possible. Peter O'Toole as

production history

Lawrence and Omar Sharif as Ali were relative newcomers to Hollywood films. *Lawrence* provided them with by far their most important roles up to this point. The two newcomers were supported by an impressive array of American and British stars. Stars recognisable to US and foreign audiences were essential to a film project as ambitious as *Lawrence*, and their involvement would have been a crucial factor in raising funding for it.

Anthony Quinn as Auda Abu Tayi was the biggest American star involved in *Lawrence*, with Jose Ferrer, Claude Rains, and Arthur Kennedy also well known. The film's two biggest British stars, Alec Guinness as Feisal and Jack Hawkins as Allenby, had worked with Lean before, most recently in *The Bridge on the River Kwai*. In keeping with the belief that an international cast would help *Lawrence* to attract audiences in as many countries as possible, French actor Maurice Ronet was initially cast in the role of Ali. Lean was dissatisfied with him, and Omar Sharif, a star of Egyptian cinema who had also done some film work in France, eventually took the role.

A section of Ella Shohat's and Robert Stam's book *Unthinking Eurocentrism* discusses 'The racial politics of casting'. Shohat and Stam identify a dominant pattern throughout Hollywood's history. White actors are cast in non-white as well as white roles, whereas non-white actors tend to be restricted to non-white roles. Anthony Quinn as Auda and Alec Guinness as Feisal are examples of this in *Lawrence*. Within the narrative, there is a contrast between these characters. Auda embodies stereotypically orientalist notions of what an Arab is like, but Feisal is a more complex Arab character who to a certain extent undermines these notions (see Ideology: Orientalism, and Ideology: Ambivalence). However, the casting of Guinness and Quinn in these roles cuts across this contrast. It implies that white actors can play any kind of non-white character, but that the reverse is not possible.

This pattern of casting continues to this day. It occurs in subsequent films directed by Lean, such as *A Passage to India* (1984). In this film Alec Guinness played an Indian character, but no Indian actors were cast as white European characters. Nevertheless, casting Omar Sharif as Ali was a bold move in the early 1960s. After *Lawrence* Sharif became the first Arab actor to attain international star status. Yet the racial politics of casting which Shohat and Stam discuss shaped his subsequent career. As an Arab actor Sharif has never been offered the same range of white *and* non-white roles that white actors like Guinness have. He has on the whole been limited to non-white roles.

Established stars bring a particular star image from their other films to the roles they are cast in. Jack Hawkins, Allenby in *Lawrence*, had previously appeared as a senior officer in a number of 1950s British war films such as *Angels One Five* (George More O'Ferrall, 1952) and *The Cruel Sea* (Charles Frend, 1953). Casting Hawkins in a similar role in *Lawrence* serves several purposes. It attracts audiences who enjoyed Hawkins's previous British military roles. *Lawrence*, though, attempts to develop a more critical perspective on the British military establishment than these earlier films did. This involves a delicate balancing act. It could be argued that casting Hawkins, a star strongly associated with decent, admirable military characters in these earlier films, effectively tones down the criticisms of the British military establishment in *Lawrence*'s narrative.

The significance of casting a particular star in a role can be analysed more precisely by applying what film theorists specialising in star studies call 'the commutation test'. This involves imagining what meanings another star, different from the one cast in the role, would have brought to a particular film. It can help to highlight the specific meanings the star who was actually cast brings to it.

The commutation test can usefully be applied to Peter O'Toole in *Lawrence*. At least two other stars, Marlon Brando and Albert Finney, were seriously considered for the role of Lawrence before O'Toole was cast. Brando decided to work on another epic, *The Mutiny on the Bounty* (Lewis Milestone, 1962). Finney's screen test was considered unsuitable. All three actors embodied new, introspective types of masculinity which became prevalent in younger American and British male star images in the 1950s and 1960s (see Cultural contexts: Audience). One way in which O'Toole differed from the other two was that he was less well known. Arguably, for audiences watching *Lawrence* when it was first released, a lack of preconceptions about its star would have heightened the character's enigmatic qualities (see Narrative circularity).

production history

REEDITING AND RESTORATION

Films often circulate in different versions and exist in different forms at different points in time. *Lawrence of Arabia* was cut quite soon after its completion because its running time was felt to be too long. Adrian Turner suggests that this was due to concerns that audiences for evening showings would miss their last buses or trains home. *Lawrence* was cut again for television screenings.

Sequences were trimmed to reduce their length, and some of the material cut from *Lawrence* also related directly to the more complex and enigmatic aspects of Lawrence's character. One example would be the shot of Lawrence's goggles hanging from a branch. This ends the opening sequence, his fatal motorcycle crash. In the restored version it is followed by a cut to Lawrence's bust in St Paul's cathedral. Colonel Brighton tells a clergyman that Lawrence was a 'remarkable chap', but admits he didn't know him very well. The goggles which have obscured Lawrence's face in the opening sequence, the direct cut to the bust of this legendary man, and Brighton's statement emphasise the difficulty of getting beyond the legend and gaining direct access to Lawrence's real motivations (see Narrative circularity). These shots were cut out of the film in the shortening process but put back in as part of the 1989 restoration.

Arguably, *Lawrence* was ahead of its time. When its running time had to be shortened, some of the film's more sophisticated and unusual moments were cut out. This turned it into a more conventional epic and minimised its 'anti-epic' aspects (see Filmography). In the mid-1980s Robert Harris, who had been involved in the restoration and rerelease of the classic silent film *Napoléon* (Abel Gance, 1927), led the effort to restore *Lawrence*. Lean and editor Anne Coates contributed to this process. Some of the original cast rerecorded lines of dialogue. *Lawrence* was rereleased, to critical acclaim, in 1989. As a result of this history of cutting and restoration, different versions of *Lawrence* have been seen at different times by different audiences. This has a bearing upon the various ways audiences have responded to the film.

impact of the intertexts

cultural contexts

INTERTEXTUALITY

The concept of 'intertextuality', derived from contemporary cultural theory, provides a useful way of analysing cultural contexts of both film production and film reception. The theory of intertextuality begins from the premise that literary or film texts do not have one fixed or unified meaning. Instead, this theory proposes that texts are always constructed by their makers (production) and understood by their audiences (reception) in relation to other texts. The originality of any specific text is defined in terms of how it refers to and combines elements from a whole range of other texts. Makers and audiences will establish connections between texts directly and indirectly, consciously and unconsciously.

Lawrence of Arabia's 'intertexts' include the narrative conventions of classical Hollywood cinema and the characteristics of the late 1950s and early 1960s 'male epic' (see Hollywood narratives, and Genre: The male epic). The film's innovative editing can be related to the French New Wave films of the late 1950s and early 1960s which *Lawrence*'s editor took as one of her points of reference. The film's complex representation of its central protagonist can be related to literary texts such as Richard Aldington's *Lawrence of Arabia: A Biographical Enquiry* which investigated the Lawrence legend during the 1950s. The disenchantment with European imperialism and militarism prevalent in much left wing political commentary after the 1956 Suez crisis also feeds into *Lawrence* (see Ideology: Ambivalence, and Production history: Script). At the same time, aspects of the film relate back to preceding literary and cinematic orientalist texts (see Ideology: Orientalism). These represent the desert as a colourful, exotic, fundamentally different world from the West, a location both enticing and dangerous for Westerners (see Ideology: Orientalism, and Ideology: The romance of the desert).

AUDIENCE

If the intertextual dimensions of *Lawrence of Arabia* are borne in mind, there can be no absolute correct or incorrect response to the film. This does not mean that every individual's response to the film is unique, or that we are all free to respond to it however we like. What it means is that different audiences in different historical and cultural contexts will tend to place more or less emphasis on different aspects of the film. Different audiences will relate the film to their own culturally and historically specific intertextual frames of reference (see Cultural contexts: Intertextuality). Even at the same point in time audiences with different interests and expectations will relate to the film differently.

To take a few examples, a fan of Hollywood epics in the early 1960s might relate primarily to the orientalist spectacle in *Lawrence*, finding it enjoyable and reassuring. Enjoyable, insofar as it is beautiful to look at. Reassuring, insofar as it reinforces the orientalist assumption that we in the West are superior to the colourful, primitive, sometimes barbarous Arabs represented in the film (see Ideology: Orientalism). A fan of the younger male stars of the 1950s and early 1960s might find Peter O'Toole's performance and Lawrence's character every bit as compelling and complex in its representation of masculinity as the roles played by James Dean, Montgomery Clift, Marlon Brando or Albert Finney during this period (see Genre: The male epic, and Production history: Casting). European or American left wing intellectuals would possibly pick up on *Lawrence's* subtle critiques of orientalism and imperialism (see Ideology: Ambivalence). An audience predisposed to read films in relation to a director's typical style and themes might look for connections between *Lawrence* and other David Lean films (see Background: Director as auteur, and Cultural contexts: Critical responses). Finally, an Arab audience might relate the film critically to historical texts by Arab writers, such as George Antonius's *The Arab Awakening* (first published in English 1938) and Suleiman Mousa's *T.E. Lawrence; An Arab View* (first published in English 1966). These give Lawrence a much less central role within the Arab revolt than the film does.

In practice these responses overlap in complex ways. It is quite possible that audiences combined more than one of the intertextual frameworks outlined above in their responses to *Lawrence*. Individual responses may change on a second or third viewing as the same viewer concentrates on different aspects of the text and relates it to different intertextual frameworks. Detailed audience research tracing the film's reception would be necessary in order to analyse these processes more precisely. Steven Caton's book on *Lawrence* contains some material on audience reception of the film in the 1960s and after the 1989 rerelease (see Production history: Reediting and restoration).

CRITICAL RESPONSES

A new wave of critical and theoretical writing on *Lawrence* emerged after the 1989 restoration of the film. The restoration literally enabled different perceptions of *Lawrence* to be formed. It focused attention on the film's 'anti-epic' aspects, and on what the director's and the other film makers' creative intentions were before the film was shortened (see Filmography, and Production history: Reediting and restoration). Simultaneously, *Lawrence's* successful rerelease demonstrated that the romance of the desert could still appeal to cinema audiences (see Ideology: The romance of the desert). Films such as *The Sheltering Sky* (Bernardo Bertolucci, 1990) and *The English Patient* (Anthony Minghella, 1997) take the superb desert location cinematography and the marginal, alienated aspects of *Lawrence's* central protagonist as one of their main points of reference (see Cinematography and mise-en-scène, and Ideology: Marginality and romantic orientalism).

Although now seen as a classic film, *Lawrence* attracted a range of critical responses when it was first released in 1962. At one end of the spectrum was Dilys Powell's lyrical enthusiasm. Other critics were less generous. Andrew Sarris, reviewing the film for the American *Village Voice*, dismissed the film as 'dull, overlong and coldly impersonal'. Sarris represented an emerging new breed of critics whose primary intertextual framework was provided by recent French critical writing on 'auteurisme' (see Background: Director as auteur).

What this new breed of critics valued most highly within Hollywood cinema was the straightforward, energetic direction of previously unacknowledged 'auteurs' such as Howard Hawks and Raoul Walsh. According to critics like Sarris, these 'auteurs' also managed to invest the often routine studio productions they worked on with their own personal themes and styles. Working on relatively low budget, low prestige productions allowed more freedom to do this, compared to epic productions like *Lawrence* which 'embalmed' directors like Lean 'in the tomb of the impersonal cinema'. Sarris argued that 'the sheer logistics', the enormous amounts of money pumped into film epics, tended to restrict the director's creative freedom. Films such as *Lawrence* were too ponderous, too self-consciously artistic, and displayed little genuine personality.

The auteurist line of thinking was developed by some influential young British critics. In 1962, the year *Lawrence* was released, the first issue of the British auteurist *Movie* magazine published a controversial 'league table' of British and American directors. The table had six categories. Howard Hawks was placed in the first category; 'great'. Raoul Walsh was one of the directors included in the second category; 'brilliant'. David Lean was placed way down in the fifth category; 'competent or ambitious'. Critics like Sarris and the *Movie* writers established which directors' work would be taken seriously within film studies for the next two decades. Yet *Lawrence* remained popular with general audiences and was shown on television. Film makers continued to regard it, in technical terms, as a landmark film. Film studies, however, tended to sideline Lean's work.

Things began to change in the 1980s. Whereas Hollywood and other European cinemas had always been taken seriously by film studies, British cinema and British directors began to be reassessed in the 1980s. An increasing concern with film history led to classic films from the past being restored and rereleased. Two films revived from the last great period of Hollywood epic production were *Spartacus* and *Lawrence of Arabia*. Both are politically sophisticated. Blacklisted Hollywood writers contributed to both films' scripts (see Production history: Script). Both films are contemporary and relevant because of the complex ways in which they represent masculinity (see Genre: The male epic). *Lawrence* also relates directly to debates within contemporary film and media studies about representations of the non-Western world (see Ideology: Orientalism). Finally, *Lawrence of Arabia* still has the power to move some viewers, like American film critic Janet Maslin, to praise it as 'the best film I know'.

bibliography

general film

Altman, Rick, *Film Genre*,
BFI, 1999
  Detailed exploration of film genres

Bordwell, David, *Narration in the Fiction Film*, Routledge, 1985
  A detailed study of narrative theory and structures

– – –, Staiger, Janet & Thompson, Kristin, *The Classical Hollywood Cinema: Film Style & Mode of Production to 1960*, Routledge, 1985; pbk 1995
  An authoritative study of cinema as institution, it covers film style and production

– – – & Thompson, Kristin, *Film Art*, McGraw-Hill, 4th edn, 1993
  An introduction to film aesthetics for the non-specialist

Branson, Gill & Stafford, Roy, *The Media Studies Handbook*, Routledge, 1996

Buckland, Warren, *Teach Yourself Film Studies*, Hodder & Stoughton, 1998
  Very accessible, it gives an overview of key areas in film studies

Cook, Pam (ed.), *The Cinema Book*, BFI, 1994

Corrigan, Tim, *A Short Guide To Writing About Film*, HarperCollins, 1994
  What it says: a practical guide for students

Dyer, Richard, *Stars*, BFI, 1979; pbk Indiana University Press, 1998
  A good introduction to the star system

Easthope, Antony, *Classical Film Theory*, Longman, 1993
  A clear overview of recent writing about film theory

Hayward, Susan, *Key Concepts in Cinema Studies*, Routledge, 1996

Hill, John & Gibson, Pamela Church (eds), *The Oxford Guide to Film Studies*, Oxford University Press, 1998
  Wide-ranging standard guide

Lapsley, Robert & Westlake, Michael, *Film Theory: An Introduction*, Manchester University Press, 1994

Maltby, Richard & Craven, Ian, *Hollywood Cinema*, Blackwell, 1995
  A comprehensive work on the Hollywood industry and its products

Mulvey, Laura, 'Visual Pleasure and Narrative Cinema' (1974), in *Visual and Other Pleasures*, Indiana University Press, Bloomington, 1989
  The classic analysis of 'the look' and 'the male gaze' in Hollywood cinema. Also available in numerous other edited collections

Nelmes, Jill (ed.), *Introduction to Film Studies*, Routledge, 1996
  Deals with several national cinemas and key concepts in film study

Nowell-Smith, Geoffrey (ed.), *The Oxford History of World Cinema*, Oxford University Press, 1996
  Hugely detailed and wide-ranging with many features on 'stars'

LAWRENCE OF ARABIA

Thomson, David, *A Biographical Dictionary of the Cinema*, Secker & Warburg, 1975
Unashamedly driven by personal taste, but often stimulating

Truffaut, François, *Hitchcock*, Simon & Schuster, 1966, rev. edn. Touchstone, 1985
Landmark extended interview

Turner, Graeme, *Film as Social Practice*, 2nd edn, Routledge, 1993
Chapter four, 'Film Narrative', discusses structuralist theories of narrative

Wollen, Peter, *Signs and Meaning in the Cinema*, Viking 1972
An important study in semiology

Readers should also explore the many relevant websites and journals. *Film Education* and *Sight and Sound* are standard reading.

Valuable websites include:

The Internet Movie Database at http://uk.imdb.com

Screensite at http://www.tcf.ua.edu/screensite/contents.html

The Media and Communications Site at the University of Aberystwyth at http://www.aber.ac.uk/~dgc/welcome.html

There are obviously many other university and studio websites which are worth exploring in relation to film studies.

the non-western world

Root, Deborah, *Cannibal Culture*, Westview Press, Boulder, Colorado, 1996
Chapter five, 'Dreams and Landscapes', discusses Western desert narratives

Said, Edward, *Orientalism: Western Conceptions of the Orient* [1978], Penguin, Harmonsworth, 1995

The classic study of European literary and scholarly representation of 'the Orient'

Shohat, Ella & Stam, Robert, *Unthinking Eurocentrism*, Routledge, 1994
The standard text on cinematic representations of the non-Western world

hollywood epic genre   bibliography

hollywood epic genre

Hunt, Leon, 'What are Big Boys Made of?', in Pat Kirkham & Janet Thumin (eds), *You Tarzan: Masculinity, Movies and Men*, Lawrence and Wishart, 1993
An analysis of representations of masculinity in Hollywood 'male epics'

Sobchack, Vivian, 'Surge and Splendor', in Barry Keith Grant (ed.), *Film Genre Reader II*, University of Texas Press, Austin, 1995
A densely written, sophisticated analysis of the Hollywood epic experience

Wood, Michael, *America in the Movies*, Basic Books, New York, 1975
Chapter eight, 'Shake the Superflux', discusses the Hollywood epic

lawrence of arabia

Anderegg, Michael, *The Films of David Lean*, Twayne, Boston MA, 1986
An auteurist analysis of Lean's films

Brownlow, Kevin, *David Lean*, Faber, 1997
The definitive biography of *Lawrence*'s director, with several chapters on the making of the film

Caton, Steven C., *Lawrence of Arabia: A Film's Anthropology*, University of California Press, Berkeley, 1999
The definitive academic analysis of the film. Caton debates some of Shohat's and Stam's comments on *Lawrence*

Hodson, Joel, 'Who Wrote *Lawrence of Arabia*?', *Cineaste* XX: 4, 1994
A discussion of Michael Wilson's and Robert Bolt's contributions to *Lawrence*'s screenplay

LoBrutto, Vincent, *Selected Takes*, Praeger, New York, 1991

Oldham, Gabriella, *First Cut*, University of California Press, Berkeley, 1992
Both books contain interviews with *Lawrence*'s editor Anne Coates

Pratley, Gerald, *The Cinema of David Lean*, Tantivy Press, London, 1974
An auteurist analysis of Lean's films

Turner, Adrian, *Robert Bolt*, Vintage, London, 1999
A biography of one of *Lawrence*'s scriptwriters

– – – *The Making of David Lean's Lawrence of Arabia*, Dragon's World, London, 1994
A lavishly illustrated account of the production and reception of the film

Young, Freddie, *Seventy Light Years*, Faber, 1999
The autobiography of *Lawrence*'s cinematographer

cinematic terms

[NB The distinctions between types of shots are general categories. It is sometimes possible to disagree about which category a particular shot falls into]

biopic a film about the life of a famous historical individual

canted framing a shot where framing is deliberately not 'level'. For example, a shot of a skyscraper where, because of canted framing, the skyscraper is at a diagonal angle

close-up a shot framing someone's face, a gesture, or an object

continuity editing system of editing which aims to keep transitions between shots as smooth as possible

crane shot a shot where the whole camera moves in any direction and leaves the ground

extreme close-up a shot magnifying a very small object, isolating a detail of an object, or isolating a part of someone's face such as mouth or eyes

extreme long shot a shot of a city or a landscape where human figures are barely distinguishable because of the size of what is included in the shot

eyeline match the direction in which an actor is looking, preparing the spectator for the direction of the next shot

long shot a shot where a person's entire body can be seen and where the background dominates

medium close-up a shot framing the human body from the chest up

medium shot a shot framing the human body from the waist up

nondiegetic music a film studies term for music on the soundtrack which does not come from a source within the narrative space

pan a camera movement where space is scanned from left to right or right to left. Short for 'panorama'

plot and story a theoretical distinction derived from the work of Russian formalist critics. The plot is the order in which story events are represented within a film's narrative. The story is the actual chronological order in which these events occurred.

representation a theoretical term used in film, media and cultural studies, referring to images analysed as cultural constructions rather than realistic or accurate reflections

screen credit acknowledgement in a film's credits sequence of a production worker's contribution to the film

shot/reverse shot a standard convention for filming conversations. A framing and editing pattern which involves alternating shots of characters facing each other. All of the shots are filmed from the same side of a line between the characters

tilt a camera movement where space is scanned from top to bottom or vice versa

track/tracking shot tracking is often used to follow complex character movements or to move into a new space. In a tracking shot the whole camera moves in any direction without leaving the ground

widescreen a format which exceeds the standard 'aspect ratio' to produce and project images in a narrower rectangle. The standard 'aspect ratio' is 1.331. For every 1 metre on the side of the frame the top and bottom have 1.33. The widescreen process Panavision could produce a ratio of 1.851

Y LAWRENCE OF ARABIA

95

credits

production company

Horizon Pictures (GB) Ltd, London, England

Released through Columbia Pictures Corporation

Première Odeon Leicester Square, 9 December 1962

director

David Lean

producer

Sam Spiegel

screenplay

Robert Bolt (and Michael Wilson)

director of photography

Freddie Young

editor

Anne Coates

art director

John Stoll

costume designer

Phyllis Dalton

production designer

John Box

music

Maurice Jarre

sound editor

Win Ryder

cast

T.E. Lawrence – Peter O'Toole

Prince Feisal – Alec Guinness

Auda Abu Tayi – Anthony Quinn

General Allenby – Jack Hawkins

Turkish bey – Jose Ferrer

Colonel Brighton – Anthony Quayle

Mr Dryden – Claude Rains

Jackson Bentley – Arthur Kennedy

General Murray – Donald Wolfit

Gasim – I.S. Johar

Majid – Gamil Ratib

Farraj – Michel Ray

Daud – John Dimech

Tafas – Zia Mohyeddin

Medical officer – Howard Marion Crawford

Club secretary – Jack Gwilliam

RAMC colonel – Hugh Miller